COURAGEOUS PATHS

STORIES OF NINE APPALACHIAN WOMEN

By
JANE B. STEPHENSON

Introduction by
GURNEY NORMAN

Afterward by
R

NEW OPPORTUNITY
SCHOOL FOR WOMEN
BEREA, KENTUCKY

Printed in the United States of America

ISBN 1-881529-09-6

Book design and typesetting by
Kimberly McGuire with assistance
from Brenda Bowlin of the
Berea College Press.

Cover design by Morris Jackson

Cover photograph is Log Cabin Quilt
from the collection of Jane B. Stephenson

Book produced by
Custom & Limited Editions
San Francisco, California

New Opportunity School for Women
204 Chestnut Street
Berea, Kentucky 40403

(859) 985-7200

www.nosw.org

DEDICATION

This book is dedicated in loving memory to my husband, John B. Stephenson, who gave me courage and inspiration to begin the New Opportunity School and this book. My great disappointment is that he did not live to see the book completed; however, he has left his own legacy to the people of Appalachia through his personal commitment and untiring efforts for the region.

ACKNOWLEDGMENTS

My special thanks to;

the women who have told their stories:

Gurney Norman, who inspired me to design the program which eventually became the New Opportunity School for Women, and for his many hours of instruction and support to participants of the School;

M. G. for transcribing hours of tapes;

Kim McGuire for preparing the manuscript for publication;

Frank Taylor, Ron Fouts, and Wilma Dykeman Stokely, who motivated and encouraged me to record and share these stories;

my children — Jennifer, Rebecca, and David — who have always been a loving source of encouragement to me;

the many people at Berea College who help make the New Opportunity School happen, especially the staff of the School;

and to the many faithful donors to the New Opportunity School.

CONTENTS

PREFACE

Many times over the years, graduates of the New Opportunity School for Women have spoken to various civic and church groups about the School. In doing so, most tell their very personal stories. The reaction of the audience is always the same: tears wiped from eyes, admiration of the courage these women have displayed in their lives over the years, and encouragement to the women to go on with their plans for changes in their lives through education and work. Many listeners ask, "Is anyone writing down these stories? They would be so inspiring for others to read."

Here you have the stories of nine women who have agreed to share their lives with you. These are very personal stories, sometimes painful to tell. In sharing these stories, some women have asked to have names and places changed in order to protect their identities and to maintain their privacy. Others have left all facts unchanged.

Although the role played by the New Opportunity School in the lives of these women is large, the object of this book is not to advertise the School but rather to show how a program such as the New Opportunity School can be life-changing for its participants. An understanding of the School is necessary in order to perceive why the women are so affected by the program.

The New Opportunity School is an outreach program of Berea College, a liberal arts school serving students from the Appalachian area of a nine-state region. Outreach into the mountain region has long been a mission of the College. The New Opportunity School extends the mission of Berea College in serving low-income, under-educated, middle-aged Appalachian women who desperately need jobs but who are without adequate knowledge of how to go about finding positions or further training.

Twice a year, fourteen women are selected to come to campus for a three-week session at no personal expense, and transportation and child care costs are also paid by the New Opportunity School. (As many women cannot arrange to leave home, job-related work-shops are also provided by the New Opportunity School in rural locations in Eastern Kentucky in order to reach women who cannot come to campus for the residential program.)

Each three-week session is filled with classes, work and cul-tural activities. During the mornings and evenings, participants attend classes on a variety of topics such as computer basics, build-ing self-esteem, creative writing, Appalachian Literature, punctua-tion skills, leadership development, how to further their education, public speaking, job search skills, women's health issues and oth-ers. In the afternoons, participants work at jobs either on campus or in the community. Weekends are spent in such cultural activities as visiting museums and attending concerts and lectures. Each woman leaves the program with a suit appropriate to wear for an interview, hair and make-up advice, and a carefully written resume. Scholarships and no-interest emergency loans are available to gradu-ates through the New Opportunity School; alumnae receive news-letters regularly and return once a year for a reunion.

The success of the women who have attended the School is phenomenal — almost seventy percent of the one hundred and eighty-nine graduates are currently employed or are enrolled in further study.

More women are coming to realize the importance of educa-tion and are determined that their own children will not drop out of school. Many children and grandchildren of our graduates are now going on to college or vocational school for more training.

A woman chosen to attend the New Opportunity School must be highly motivated, have a GED or high school diploma, and agree to stay the entire three weeks. Once a woman is chosen, it is sometimes difficult for her to arrange for baby sitters and get the needed support of her family to be away for three weeks. Many have never been away from family and community, so it is a frightening step to take. Typical questions passing through their minds are: Will my husband let me come? Can I survive on a college campus? Will I like my roommate? Can I do the work assigned to me? Will I get homesick? Can my children survive without me? Can I survive without them? Will this program really make a difference in my life?

Once the women have arrived on campus, adjusted to being away from home, and mastered their hectic schedules, they begin to realize they are quite capable of accomplishing much more than they had ever thought possible. For example, most are surprised at how easy it is to learn to use a computer and are very proud to leave with professional resumes they themselves have written on computers.

Building self-esteem is one of the most important goals of the program — and one of the most needed. Many of the women in the program have been abused, told they are worthless, or told they can't do anything right. Some have been mistreated by the very systems that should be helping them — agencies they go to for help when they have no one else to turn to. Most have not travelled far from home and finding that they can do so with ease is a great boost to their self-esteem. Meeting new people and well-known writers such as Wilma Dykeman, Gurney Norman, and the late Alex Haley increases their ability to be comfortable with new people in new situations.

The personal care and concern for each woman by the staff of the New Opportunity School as well as the faculty and staff of Berea College often surprises the participants. While in the School they feel nourished and loved in an atmosphere created for their well-being. This is an ideal situation for learning, for growing, for taking time to sort out lives and set realistic goals for the future. It is also a time to talk and learn from each other. Sometimes returning home from the School can be very difficult and the cause of family problems, as you will learn from several stories in this book.

As you read about these nine women, you may be sure that there are many more with similar stories and similar successes. You will weep; you will rejoice in their happiness; and you will be angered by the injustices in their lives. Most of all, you will be impressed by their courage, their tenacity, their determination to make significant changes.

Those of us who work with the New Opportunity School feel privileged to know these special women and to experience a small part of their lives. Sharing their success is a continuing joy. Grieving with them in their disappointments is often difficult. Knowing them is always a blessing.

Jane B. Stephenson, Director
New Opportunity School for Women
Berea College
Berea, Kentucky
August, 1995

INTRODUCTION

"Eventually You Will See A Light"

Twice a year for nearly a decade I have participated as a writing teacher in Berea College's New Opportunity School for Women. The New Opportunity School is an intensive three-week course in which every hour of every day is packed with scheduled activities for the fourteen women who attend. I meet only twice with the group for an hour and forty five minutes each session. Some of our writing exercises concern fictional techniques but our main focus is on personal narrative writing. The idea is to use our class time to make pencils move across pages, putting words on paper, practicing writing instead of talking about it.

On the face of it, it would seem that not much can happen, writing-wise, in only two meetings, but the fact is, we accomplish a great deal. The first couple of times I worked with the New Opportunity School women I didn't understand how they could write so much, and from such emotional depth, in so little time. Then I realized that this writing group has a unique advantage: for twenty one straight days, the women are in conversation with each other many hours of every day, and much of that conversation is personal story telling. The New Opportunity School offers its members many valuable things in three weeks but perhaps the most precious is the opportunity to talk in depth with other women whose life experiences parallel their own.

Our writing sessions, then, are occasions for the women to write down the stories they have been telling to each other and, through the act of writing, to discover yet more stories to tell. Speaking and writing, writing and telling, reading in order to hear. These are verbal arts. To be with these women in living practice of these arts, and in earnest discussion of serious life-matters of the kind on display in this book, is always a great pleasure for me, and a great honor as well. Many times I have arrived in Berea for my two-day stint with the New Opportunity School feeling weary and dispirited from the stresses of my own life, wondering if I have enough available psychic energy to conduct a writing workshop. But always, as soon as our class begins and we start to talk, and then to write and then to read aloud what we have written, I feel my energy returning. The spirit and language and wit and wisdom of the women who attend the New Opportunity School create an atmosphere that feels like home to me and I always go away completely restored.

Until the publication of this book I have had no way to explain to friends that certain quality the women of the New Opportunity School possess and share with anyone in their vicinity. The stories in this book, and the sound of the voices that tell them, make this quality, which is rooted in the thoughts and experiences of these women, accessible in a rare way.

It isn't easy to put into words the awesome experience of struggling for simple survival in circumstances of such palpable insecurity that the struggling person can see no way out. The sense of being in quicksand is almost impossible to convey to people standing on dry land. People in deprived circumstances are usually invisible to people who are not. Like veterans of frontline combat in war, most survivors of such extreme life situations usually don't have much to say about it. I have often thought that it is useless to even try to describe this side of life to the uninitiated, in the grim conviction that no verbal description, no matter how brilliantly stated, can ever make a dent in the consciousness of people who have not experienced it firsthand. But the women whose words fill this book prove me wrong. They have lived life to the full and then found within themselves the strength to believe their experiences are important and the language to make their lives known to others.

In their lives these women have rarely found encouragement to value their own stories and to own their own creative power. The women who have attended the New Opportunity School at Berea College give much credit to the School for helping them along their path. This credit is well deserved. Berea College's long tradition of offering educational opportunity to people of humble background has no peer in this country. In the end, though, all who work with the women of the New Opportunity School know that it is the innate qualities of the women themselves that give this unique program its special vitality.

Different readers will of course find different meanings in the stories that are told here. No one comes to the act of reading empty-handed or empty-headed or innocent. Some bring garbled projections to the act of reading; others bring their own relentless agendas. It is my hope that readers will receive these stories in the same open and generous spirit in which they are offered. The forthright honesty of these speakers is plain for all to see. Compared to the shallow ideas, the devious language and general mean-spiritedness that characterize the nation's public discourse in these times, the dignified manner of the women who address us here is as refreshing as a drink of cold water from a mountain spring.

The narratives you will read on the following pages describe some of the hardest experiences that people must endure in life. Poverty, deprivation, separation from loved ones, loss of home and family, illiteracy, unemployment, sickness, lack of medical care, social exclusion, hardship, dominance by men, abuse by men, death of loved ones are running themes throughout these narratives. But these stories speak of more than the pain and suffering of life. They speak of love, loyalty, struggle, effort, sacrifice. They speak of strength, endurance, defiance, determination and triumph. They also speak of education, coming to knowledge, of advancing on in life to greater maturity and understanding and individual autonomy. One of the things I appreciate most about these stories is the way the speakers display their hard-won strength and maturity by refusing to sound like victims as they recount their difficult lives. Anyone with preconceptions about women with stories such as these will be frustrated by their refusal to accept any roles that others with agendas may want to assign to them. If these women were ever at one time vulnerable to the manipulations of others, these narratives show that that time is now over. In telling us their stories these graduates of the New Opportunity School ask for our attention in a confident way and then become teachers to us all.

Near the end of her narrative Ada says, "I would say to other women in my situation to do the best that you can do. Maybe you don't see no way out. But as long as you keep on a-pushing and working on yourself, eventually you will see a way out. Eventually you will see a light." It is not just women who have known hard times who need to pay attention to Ada's words. Ada and her New Opportunity School sisters who have spoken in this book have a valuable message for our times. Surrounding these immediate speakers are one hundred and eighty-nine other women who have attended the New Opportunity School whose life-stories are just as compelling as these. Hopefully the examples of these bright, articulate, courageous people will show many others that their lives and experiences are valuable and that, indeed, "eventually you will see a light."

Gurney Norman

EVELYN

We lived in a place called Blue, Kentucky. It was a very isolated community — most of the people on the mountain remained on that mountain. I was born over at the Pattie A. Clay Hospital and shortly after I was born the house on the mountain which my mom and dad owned at the time — just an old-timey construction — burnt down. There was no electricity, water, anything like that.

My father was quite old when I was born. He was in his late fifties or early sixties and my mom was in her forties. My father had three kids by a previous marriage — two boys and a girl. Then him and my mom were married and there was six besides me. I was the youngest and most of them were grown by the time I come along.

Mom was illiterate — she didn't read or write. If she could've read and all, maybe she would have had a chance at a job. She didn't drive and there was no work available anywhere near where we lived because we lived away from town. She had no transportation and her health wouldn't have held up even if she could have gotten a job. She had it rough trying to raise us. Dad would go up to Jackson County, up in the mountains and cut logs. See, Dad didn't pay in enough to have Social Security. The man that he worked for took it out of his pay but didn't turn it in.

Mom was originally from Owsley County and Dad was from around Owsley County somewhere. I'm not sure exactly where but later on when he got married the first time he took his wife and moved to Michigan. That's where he lived until he got divorced from her. He moved back and that's when he met Mom. Dad at one time worked for the railroad making the hubs for the trains — he was a blacksmith.

We stayed within the mountain area for several years and then moved off the mountain and down into Jackson County. Mom and Dad would get abandoned houses because they didn't have the money to pay rent, and I don't think they had government housing projects at that time. So, we lived mainly in abandoned houses where the rent was practically nothing or the landlord didn't care whether he got any rent or not. One place we moved to the flood water washed one of the neighboring houses out. The backwater would come right up to the house, so we had to leave it. Most of the houses we lived in during the winter when you had to build fires, well, they would burn down. They wasn't in very good shape at all. There was no running water, no electricity — we used kerosene.

That was from about 1959 to 1963. Then in 1963, Daddy died. Mom moved us to Georgetown for a while where my oldest sister lived. And things didn't work out too good — they didn't get along. Mom moved us back up on the mountain where there was an old log cabin called the Baird place. We lived in it for two or three years and it was exactly that — a log cabin. It, too, was ready to fall down but I guess a good point of it was that within a few feet of the house was Dad's grave. When things got real bad, I would walk up on the mountain to the gravesite and sit there and talk to Daddy. It helped to survive the mountain itself.

We walked to school a mile and a half each way. We went to a one-room school with eight grades in it. We had a teacher that come in from town and we had books that was donated to the school for a library. I would say there was about forty of us going to the one-room schoolhouse. My other sisters and brothers were grown and had gotten married at this point except for one sister.

School started at seven-thirty in the morning and was out at four o'clock. There were no buses as most of the kids that went to the school were in closer range than we were but we was way back in the holler so it was a little bit more difficult to get to school. Most of the time Mom managed to get us shoes in the winter and in the summer we went barefoot. There was no jackets and no coats and by the time we got to school we was usually froze to death. We had an old pot-bellied stove in the center of the schoolroom. We would get around it and get warm after we got there. The teacher would have the kids in the eighth grade help the ones in the smaller grades, because she had difficulty teaching eight grades of school.

Each day three sixth, seventh and eighth grade girls took turns preparing dinner for all of us. The teacher would rotate it so it would be three different girls each day. We had a little kitchenette in the school and they would prepare food and we would eat it on paper plates. They didn't have food stamps back then but a lot of the food was brought in and distributed by the government. We had potatoes and stuff like that and the girls would cook the meat from the commodities in with the potatoes. We had paper plates but they still had to wash the pots and pans. The rest of the kids would remain in the class.

There was a real close inter-relationship with all the kids. Everybody knew everybody and nobody made fun of anybody or put anybody down because we was all from the same neck of the woods. I went to school there from the third through fifth grades.

Now when I moved out into the city schools, it was a lot different. Mom moved us off the mountain and back into town because it was in the winter-time and we couldn't get in or out to get to town and buy food or anything. Mom found us a place in town where we lived until I got married. I went to the city schools and it was very difficult to adjust to the bigger school. You know, I felt totally lost. The kids were different. There was different categories of kids — you had the middle class, the upper class and then the lower class. It was real hard to see people different because I was so used to everybody being the same. And the teachers were a lot different, too. The one at the mountain school was just an average, typical housewife — motherly type — a lady. But the ones at the city school were little, petite, well-dressed, very professional types of persons. That was more of a distraction because you would sit there and envy them rather than concentrate on things.

I guess out of the whole school, we was probably the poorest of the poor. I remember one year when I was in the third grade, I had a maroon colored coat with a fox collar on it which would be in great style today. Our house had burned and that coat was given to us by somebody in the community as a donation because the clothes and everything we had had burned up. Well, when I wore the coat to school, I was tickled to death to have it. I didn't have a coat to start with. The teacher that I had at that time hung that coat outside in the snow because she said it was smelling up the rest of the coats. I wore my coat home and it froze me to death where it had hung outside. I never forgave her for it — I never forgot it either.

Now, if I see a family burned out or in need or read in the paper where families have been burned out, I send them clothes or I'll send food. I don't believe in kicking somebody because they're down. Some people may be able to do better but they don't choose to. A lot of times, though, it's cases where people are doing the best they can do.

I liked school very much. When I could get over being poor, I did well. A lot of times when a child is mis-treated because it's poor, it doesn't mean that it's not human. And it feels. A lot of the time when people are making fun of you and are putting you down, it is hard to concentrate on what you are there for. There's so much hurt inside and you keep it all bottled in until you withdraw from everything.

My sister, she got straight A's. She blocked out everything anyone ever said to her and she went on and done her work. That was her way of showing them that she was good. I didn't comprehend that. I was shy and real awkward and backward and anything anybody done to me I was so sensitive, I just broke down. I was a very nervous child; I let what they said and did control me more than she did. She would have the teachers the year before I would and when I didn't do too good the teachers would say, "Well, why can't you be like her?" I tried so hard to be like her that I couldn't be myself. Later on we went to different schools where the people couldn't relate us and I was judged for myself and not what they expected me to be.

My father, he was seventy-two and blind when he died. I was nine years old. He made ax handles and walking canes and he done a beautiful job on them. He would set and whittle them out first and then he would sand them down. He would cut wedges in them and take a pry bar and hold the wood open and I would drop marbles in the walking canes for him.

He was a big old man — he never dressed fancy. He wore bibbed overalls and plaid shirts and old work shoes, and people would make fun of him. Back then, there wasn't free lunches — most of the time our lunch cost a quarter but we didn't have that quarter. Mom would threaten to whip us if we did eat lunch because the teachers had got so nasty about us charging so many times and not having the money to pay it. Dad would walk to town and sell ax handles and walking canes in the courthouse yard and then he would bring our lunch money to the school. Well, the other kids would snicker and laugh and make fun of Dad. That done something to me. Daddy loved his kids. He showed that he did — I never saw other parents walking to the school and bringing the kids lunch money.

Dad had had a heart attack and they took him to the hospital while I was at school. We got to bring him home for a couple of days then he went back to the hospital but he never came back home — he died in the hospital. Within ten months, Mom took sick. She woke us up about two in the morning throwing up all this blood — it was hideous. I cried and begged her not to go to the hospital because I was afraid that she wouldn't be coming back, too. So, she wouldn't leave. That night, the ambulance come after her. They tried to get her to go that night, but she wouldn't so they said they would be back in the morning after her. The next morning, they come and got her and the doctors told us that the chance of her living wasn't much. All her veins had collapsed and she had lost so much blood. Not only was she vomiting the blood, but the blood was coming through the pores of her skin. They took out three-fourths of her stomach.

When Mom got so sick my oldest sister tried to take care of us younger two. It was very difficult for her as far as managing, seeing that we were at school and were being treated right, paying what little bills we had, trying to get food in the house. Mainly the only food that we had was what we got from the commodities. Of course, you had to manage to get into town and try to pick it up, try to get back to where Mom was at and to be with her. My sister was more the mother to me than my mother was because Mom wasn't able to do much. I was nine at the time and my sister was about seventeen. It was very difficult for her.

Mom stayed in the hospital three or four weeks — it was a long time. Then we took her back home, and I remember it was in the winter time and the ambulance had a horrible time getting there with her. They put her on a specific diet, very little could she eat. She sneaked out and got a biscuit and ate it and she started bleeding. So we had to call the ambulance and have them come and take her back. It was just nightmarish. But, as far as providing for us, I think Mom done the very best she could, considering. You look at the times now and a lot of people think we have it hard. If you put yourself in Mom's position, with kids, I don't think any of us could probably have done much better. She had nothing to do with. It's just like putting a totally handicapped, no-armed, no-legged person out there in the world and saying "survive." Basically that's what she was — being an illiterate, not being able to write, nor drive. No money was coming in. For a lot of people now there's the Social Security or welfare for them if they're widowed. But we didn't have that. It made us strong in a lot of ways.

So, after she had to go back to the hospital because she was bleeding again, she stayed two or three weeks that time. We went to my oldest sister's. She lived in Richmond and had eight kids of her own. We went to stay with her so that it wouldn't be so difficult for us to come to see Mom as she was in the hospital in Richmond then. We stayed there until Mom got back on her feet, but she never did physically recover. Her health never got back up to standard level. The most I've ever known my mom to weigh was like one hundred and fifteen pounds.

My dad's only sister, she was real old. She lived over in Jackson County and they had an empty house. It was old, but we moved into it to take care of my aunt. It eventually burnt down shortly after we moved out of it. She was diabetic and her relatives made a deal with us that we could have free rent if we would stay and take care of her at night. We done that for a long time and I went to school there. She was real hard to handle, a difficult person to live with.

While we were living there, the oldest of us three girls had gotten married and that didn't go over well. Mom didn't approve

6

of the girls dating and my sister was nineteen or twenty years old, but Mom didn't like the guy that she married and wouldn't let my sister have none of her clothes — she run her off. Mom was a vicious little stick of dynamite when she got mad. It was a long time before my sister was allowed to come back home, and that distraught me because my sister was my mother-figure. If I got hurt, it was her I went to and she brushed my hair. She was the one that washed my clothes and ironed them — I can see her now standing over an old ironing board. She would heat them old cast-iron irons on the stove all day long. That was how she ironed the clothes — made homemade starches and starched my things. They wasn't fancy, but she kept them clean.

After my mom and my sister and I moved from my aunt's house things got hard. We moved into a house where we was paying one hundred and thirty-five dollars a month rent and the utilities. Then it got to a point to where Mom had started getting welfare on us kids, but it wasn't enough to pay the bills. Somebody had to work so I went to work in a restaurant making ninety-five cents an hour plus tips. I was thirteen. Then I went to work at a truck stop where a job for waitresses paid more than what I was making so I went to work there. It was third shift. I'd work eleven to seven and then I'd get home between seven thirty and eight in the morning, change clothes and be at school by eight. The principal had found out that I was working at the truck stop and he told me that I could either quit work or quit school as that wasn't the kind of job that a reputable student would have. It was either work and have clothes to wear to school and help Mom with the bills or quit work, starve, not have nothing and still not be able to go to school. So I quit school so my oldest sister could continue. She was the only one out of seven of us kids that graduated from high school.

So when I was thirteen I quit school and worked awhile at the truck stop then went back to the restaurant that I had worked at before. They gave me more money on the hour. I was what they called a "car hop." I would go out to the cars and take orders then go back in and bring the food out.

Well, this guy drove in to the restaurant and he asked to drive me home. I really couldn't afford a taxi so I let him take me home. Most of the time if you called a taxi when you was working at the restaurant they would proposition you in trade for their cab rides. Or, the girls were hassled until they got home, but it was either that or walk. So, I let this guy take me home and Mom went off the deep end. Shortly thereafter, Mom started beating on me — Mom was very violent. To Mom, if a girl even looked at a man, she was in the wrong — was bad, was indecent. It was just the old-fashioned way. There's a lot of kids still raised that way today — a lot of parents feel that way. But back then, even if you was twenty years old, to my mom, you did not look at a man because if you did you was being bad. We wasn't allowed to date. If we had a boy to come and set and watch TV, she would sit right in the room with us. We couldn't hold hands or do nothing — you were friends — you sat across the room from each other.

About a week after he had brought me home he come back to the restaurant and took me home. She started beating me, and he said, "Never again." We decided at that time to get married. That was on a Thursday and on the following Friday, we got married. I didn't even know what his last name was — I looked at my marriage license to see what his name was. He had already pulled three or four years in Vietnam so he was quite a few years older than me. The only reason Mom signed for me to marry him was because she thought he had a lot of money. She thought it would make things easier, but he wasn't even working at the time — he didn't even have a home. His mom had died with cancer while he was in Vietnam. He had been living with his mom in a place down in the holler and since she died while he was gone, he didn't have a home. He had to move in with his brother and his wife and their two kids. He was sharing a bedroom with the kids and it was causing difficulties so we just decided to get married and keep a home together. He'd have a place and I'd have a place. Big dreams and no money. But we made it for sixteen years.

He took me to Louisville. To me that was like going to California or someplace like that. He rented us a little old one bedroom apartment down there and he went to work with his brother in construction. I did not go outside — I was petrified I guess.

I was almost eighteen when I delivered our first child. I had had several miscarriages before and the doctor said a lot of it had to do with undernourishment and not being well-developed during

8

childhood. My son weighed five pounds, ten ounces when he was born but he lost down to three pounds and he almost died — but he's six foot tall now. Two years later, my daughter was born.

We stayed in Louisville until our first child was born. My husband got very dominant as the marriage went on — he said he married me young so he could raise me the way he wanted me to be. I wasn't allowed out of the house — my job was to stay in and clean up, take care of the two babies. We had finally moved into the government projects in Georgetown. We had tile floors and I had to go over them with brillo pads every Saturday morning, every floor, and they had to have three coats of wax on them. The kids had to be bathed and cleaned up and everything in A-l shape by noon. If I had that done, he would take me to my sister's out in the country. That was my outing for the week. When you took your shoes off, you set them side by side, toe to toe — everything had to be just so-so. He done all the grocery shopping. If the kids needed shoes and stuff, he would come up with the money. I very seldom ever got outside the house. I cleaned house, cooked supper, took care of the kids, fixed his breakfast, washed dishes, washed and ironed curtains the old fashioned way, done laundry — most of the time on the old wringer type washer. At the time, I felt that was the way it was supposed to be, because that's the only way I had ever known. But the more I saw of how friends' relationships was and how things was with them, the more it dawned on me that something was wrong with mine.

We was living in Georgetown and he was driving back and forth to Cincinnati doing construction work. I tried working at hospitals and stuff, but it didn't work out. He was very jealous. I didn't drive at the time. I've always been petrified of cars because my brother was an alcoholic and when he got drunk, his main thrill was to get you in the car and see how fast he could go with you. He decided to show me how fast a car would go when he got drunk and angry and it put a fear in me against cars. So I never would learn how to drive and it wasn't until I was twenty-six years old that I went and got my driver's license.

Once I started driving, taking some freedom, I would go somewhere even when my husband wasn't at home. I would sneak out and try to get back and park the car so that he wouldn't know that

I had moved it. He had always told me I was dumb, stupid, igno-rant and I couldn't do nothing. Anything he handed out I had to take because I was too dumb to be able to make it. Once somebody has drilled that into you for so long, it takes a long time for some-body else to convince you otherwise.

I had always wanted to go back to school. As a matter of fact, I was very jealous and I had a lot of anger at my sister because she finished high school and I didn't. A lot of time, she would throw it up to me. It was hard enough to know that I had give up something of myself in order for her to have it and now I'm getting flack from her because I gave to her. It didn't seem fair. I had always wanted to go back to school — there was so many things to do if I just had the education. I would go and apply for jobs at Manpower and other places and stand in line for hours and get up to the window and they'd say, "Well, I'm sorry, I can't take your application — you don't have a high school degree."

I remember one time in the winter, I stood in a line at a factory for hours with both babies to put in an application and got up to the front and they wouldn't let me on in. I got angry. I started talking with this girl, Sheila. She was going to college at the time, to East-ern Kentucky University. I envied her so much. She said, "Well, why don't you go get your GED?" I said, "I can't pass it. I barely got a sixth grade education. I've not even finished grade school."

This was before my divorce. Getting divorced wasn't the easi-est thing in the world I ever done because I had never been on my own at all. It had got to the point where we stayed in debt. Our rent wasn't paid; our utilities wasn't paid. I went to work in restau-rants because that was the only kind of work I could get, but at least it was bringing something in. I worked third shift so that I wouldn't have to pay a babysitter. I would save my tips all week long — I would hide them back — I would put them in my purse and when I would get my paycheck at work I would take my tips and check home. While I was asleep, he had taken my money out of my purse and drank it up. One of the most embarrassing times in my life was to go through a grocery store line and then realize that I didn't have any cash to pay for it. I got to a point to where the kids were hun-gry, and I got tired of worrying about whether we were going to have a place to live the next day or not. I never knew what was next.

There was lots of times in the earlier part of our marriage that there was no work for him. He would go a year at a time and wouldn't work. When my kids were very young, he up and sneaked out in the middle of the night and left with my brother and went to Texas. I had no idea where he was gone — that he was even gone. There was no money. I went to my sister-in-law — she lived in the same project that I lived in. I figured he was down there talking to my brother, so I took the baby and went down there. She said, "He ain't here. He left this morning — they left for Texas."

His brother was, I guess what you'd call a wino — he'd drink anything going or coming. If it could be drank, if it was in liquid form, he would drink it. He was living with us — we all the time had other people living with us. My brother was an alcoholic; my husband was an alcoholic; his brother was an alcoholic, and they all come to stay with us. Nobody worked — I done all the cooking, the cleaning, the washing, everything for all of them. One of them was very abusive to me, but I would lie to my husband and tell him I walked into the door facing. We shared a bathroom with another couple so I'd tell him they left the door open. At that time I was pregnant with the set of twins that was born dead because of the beating I took.

My brother who was living with us, he was a drifter. He would drift in and out. He would go for years and we'd never hear from him. But when he did come in — he was mean, he was a cruel person. He eventually got sent to the penitentiary for bootlegging up in the mountains where I was born. When he got out of prison, he was even more violent than he ever was. He still drifted in and out but when he would come in, he always expected us to take care of him. He was never responsible for his own self — he was a professional bum and was good at it. He was also an alcoholic. He'd been in several mental institutions we found out about several years after his death. One morning at my sister's house he took a fourteen gauge shotgun and blew his heart out at the kitchen table. My brother-in-law and sister was in the stripping barn stripping tobacco and he had went up there shortly after breakfast for a little while and had come back to the house where the rest of us was in the living room watching "Tuxedos". It sounded like firecrackers that

11

had gone off. He was dead when we got there and he had left a twelve page suicide note that we had no idea he had even written — we found it on the bed. What my brother had done is put the stock of the gun down on the floor and leaned over the barrell and triggered it with his toe. The coroner came out and when they found the suicide note they asked about the gun. Everybody told them that my brother-in-law did rush in and unload the gun because there was a bunch of kids around.

My younger brother, he never got over that. Him and my brother were close, you know. They drank together and fit together and everything else, but they were still close. And for some reason the directors at the funeral home let him go down and look at my brother's body where the wound was. He had nightmares for years over that, so he set hisself up to be killed on my other brother's birthday. He was dating a girl up in the mountains and he had kept after me to take him up there. I talked to him all night long to try to keep him from going up there because I told him it was only trouble. But nothing else would do him, so after I got my son off to school, I took him up there. He called her and told her he was coming up there. Well, when we got to the restaurant where she worked he went in and him and her got into it. What he didn't know was that she had called her previous boyfriend, a cop, and told him that he was threatening her. The cop came and my brother was killed. They tried to get me for conspiracy some way, because he had told me earlier that she would either do what he said or he'd kill her — or some off-the-wall comment like that. Men are all the time handing you that line. You very seldom ever take them serious. The cops said that I knew about it; therefore, it was a conspiracy, but they finally released me to come back and I went and got my son out of school. I had to go identify the body that was brought back. From that point on, I never remembered nothing. I never recalled any-thing — it was just a mental block and I went for years, trying to remember. It took me years of re-adjustment and I finally said, "Look, I felt responsible because I took him up there." He was thirty-six years old — several years older than I was. It took a lot of look-ing at it to finally realize that he was responsible for his actions and the only thing I was responsible for was mine — he asked me to take him somewhere and I did. There comes a point in time when the responsibilities for our actions have to lie where they belong; we've got to quit feeling guilty for what other people do because it will destroy you. He was a grown man; he knew what he was walking into and I think he planned it. I think he wanted to die that day and I think that's why he called her when he left here. I think that's why he wanted me there — he didn't want to die alone without anybody there — any family.

It was like that all my life. I mean, growing up I remember constant battles. My sister's husband didn't work; he didn't read or write and all he could do was farming or tobacco — so a lot of times, they didn't have money. Then everybody would come back home to Mama's, and the only food we had was what we raised in the garden. A lot of times I've took the grubbing hoe and made the rows and planted beans and tomatoes and stuff and raised a garden. The last two years I had a garden that was more for my own benefit because I enjoyed being outdoors and I liked to feel the dirt and to watch things grow. You've accomplished something and I think that's what I always wanted to do, was accomplish something. Only thing is, I've been told all my life I wasn't no good at nothing.

By the time my kids was like thirteen and ten, I took the kids and filed for divorce. My husband was the only person in my life that didn't physically abuse me. Mentally, he destroyed me, but physically he didn't hurt me. I finally convinced him that our relationship was more like brother/sister. We were very protective of each other, very loving to each other that way. But as husband and wife, we just wasn't. We were more friends; we had the relationship that a person should have with a brother or a sister and I valued that. I convinced him that we would both be better off to split, be friends, him have a life with somebody that cared about him the way he should be cared for and me the way I should be. And we agreed. We had a friendly conversation and talked, but it never dawned on me that he was actually leaving. I got up one morning and asked him why he didn't go to work and he said, "I'm moving out today." What I didn't know was that he already had another female lined up, which was fine with me.

With the divorce and everything, there was no food or nothing when he left. My son's birthday was shortly after he left. I ended up with about three hundred dollars worth of food sitting in my kitchen floor on my son's birthday. Somebody had called the churches and they would never tell me who sent the food. There was about six carloads of food come to my house that day. I didn't have any money to buy my son anything for his birthday so I said, whatever you want for supper, I'll fix it if it takes me all night. He picked out fish sticks and french fries and that was what we had for supper. They brought enough food that I know it done us three months. I have no idea who done it because I didn't talk to anybody — nobody in my neighborhood even knowed that he was gone, moved out. I kept to myself — I've always been that way.

Anyway, after he left I couldn't keep the trailer going because he was giving me like two hundred dollars a month for the kids. That wasn't enough for me to make it. I got a job at Olan Mills for a little while, but it wasn't paying anything. It was phone soliciting, so you didn't really make anything. I went to work at a tobacco warehouse, third shift and moved into the project. Well, when I went to work, ninety percent of what I made the landlord took. He had a key and would come into the apartment any time he wanted to.

I had moved Mom in with me because nobody else would take care of her — I was the only choice left. The doctors told us if she lived by herself she wouldn't make it. She was almost dead when I found her; I went up to check on her and she was real ill, she had double pneumonia. The rest of the kids refused to take care of her, so I had to — I mean it was either that or put her in a nursing home which she didn't want to go to. She was of sound mind, so you couldn't force her. I took her when I was in the middle of the divorce and moved her in with me. All we had at that time was her check and the child support, and it took most of that for rent. At that time, Mom was able to get around, but she just couldn't be by herself because the pneumonia had destroyed her lungs so bad and she had emphysema too. Her heart was real bad — she had been on heart medication for years.

I found a house for three hundred and fifty dollars a month. A friend of mine went with me and signed the lease with me saying if I couldn't pay it, he would. Then I went to work at a nightclub. I started waitressing and I ended up being the assistant manager. I would cook supper for the family before I left for work and I'd work until three or four in the morning.

There would be some nights that I would make as much as three hundred dollars in tips alone, but my paycheck was lousy. I was the highest server that they had as far as drinks go — one night I served like nine hundred dollars worth of drinks.

I was totally beat when I got home. But I would save my tips all week long, and then when it got time to pay my bills as they would come in, I would take it out of my tips. I survived — I made it. I was making it better, actually, than my ex-husband was and he was making three times more in a month than I was. He got angry at first when the child payments got upped by a judge — but he has never been late with it. He's been very good about supporting the kids. We're good friends and he comes over for the kids' birthday parties and stuff like that. Basically, our relationship now is like it always was — more of a friendship.

The nightclub closed down and it was shortly after that that my friend, Sheila, made the appointment for me to take the GED test. It took several years of her talking to me and coaxing me and telling me that I could do it. Bless her heart, she went to the vocational school and sat in the classroom with me while I took the classes for the GED test. She practically led me through it. I was so pleased when I passed it. As soon as I got the GED I went back to vocational school, where I took typing. After I got done with it, I went to a business course and while I was attending it, I saw in the paper that applications were being taken for the New Opportunity School. So I applied for it.

My friend, Sheila, applied for the New Opportunity School too. Then she was accepted and I wasn't. I had built so much into coming to that school that it was like a disaster when I got the letter saying I couldn't come. Once I got the GED I felt like nothing could stop me. I felt I had to keep going — I could do anything that was available to me. That's the kind of feeling it gives you when you accomplish something like that. Well, I called the New Opportunity School and told them if there was a cancellation I would be interested in coming. And, sure enough, there was a cancellation. I went and talked to them at the secretarial school and they gave me a leave, providing I made up the work that I missed the three weeks that I was at the New Opportunity School.

While I was in the New Opportunity School, the honesty of all the girls was important to me. When you come into a program like that, you have very low self-esteem, especially if you are from the Appalachian area. You think that you are the only one in the world like that and you want to keep that part of your life a secret. Then I came to the school and we had classes in literature about Appalachia. A lot of people don't seem to understand that there is still people out there today that is still in the same place I was thirty-five years ago. It helps you to build your own self-esteem up and have confidence in yourself when you spend a period of time with a group of women that is more or less of the same category that you're in. You can relate to these people. Most people that you know on a daily basis, they're not the kind who've been where you've been and they don't understand, so you don't relate to them. In this group of women, you've become friends — you remain friends throughout from that day on. It's very hard the first day to open up and it's very nerve-wracking because you are very frightened. It's like a baby when it takes its first step — it's scared to death, but it gets up and takes that second step. And that's the way a lot of women are when they first start the program, but when they leave, they are like a different group of women altogether.

After the New Opportunity School, I went back to finish up the secretarial course and shortly after that I went back to the vocational school and took data processing. As soon as I finished that, I went to Eastern Kentucky University, where I started attending college and I've been going there ever since. Up to this point I have been carrying a B average. When I first started at Eastern Kentucky University I went nine hours the first semester. The classes are not hard. Actually, it's very understandable material and it's something that I dearly love. I am in criminology and police administration. I'm reading it and doing the work, but my mind is absorbed in other things. There's a lot of personal things that are effecting my concentration.

You see, my mother was living with me and was not well. I was working and taking care of children and taking classes and then I got acquainted with my present husband through my daughter. She was about thirteen and he had taught her how to swim at a pool where my sister-in-law lived and I had no idea that he was even in existence. Finally, I told her that I had to meet him some-time. After my divorce had become final, we started dating and ended up getting married. She lets me know quite often if it wasn't for her, I would never have got him — I owe it all to her.

For awhile his mom was living with us too. She had Alzheimer's disease and she got to the point to where she would go up into the front yard and get out in the road. It got to where if we went in another room, it would take her about two seconds to get gone. She would be out in the middle of the road and she would see a car and she didn't relate it as going to run over her or harm her. She thought it was taking her somewhere. We had to put her in a nursing home, but for a year, I had both our moms and was still going to school.

Last August, my mother died. Mama had been in the hospital. She had dehydrated, which was pretty common for her, so when I brought her into the hospital, they run x-rays and seen that she had a spot on her lung and they confirmed that it was lung cancer. They built her back up through IV's and got her to where I could take her home. They said that it would probably be about six months before the effects of the cancer would start showing. In four months, she was dead.

She wanted to die at home. She talked to me about dying at home and at first I told her I'd have to think about it because I had the kids there and, of course, my husband and me. I didn't know how I could handle her dying at home. I talked to the doctor and he said that with it being in her lungs and the condition that she was in, the chances was she would just go to sleep and not wake up — her lungs would just collapse and she would die in her sleep, peace-fully.

Well, it didn't turn out that way because the cancer moved on into her kidneys, into her liver and into her brain. The last three weeks was excruciating pain for her. She got to the point to where she couldn't talk. Her body had already stiffened out two weeks before she died and she got a horrible discoloration to her.

Mom's doctor set up this hospice and home-health to come in and help me. But Mom had made me promise that when it got real bad for her that I would not leave her, that I would be the one to take care of her because she never wanted to go back into a hospital. I don't know why unless it's because they had taken her cigarettes. Mom was a smoke fanatic. They had taken her cigarettes away from her, which, at the age of seventy-eight, that's all she had left was her cigarettes. At that point, they couldn't have done her any more harm.

Anyway, she made me promise that I would not leave her, and I didn't. So, day and night for three weeks, I sat by her bed. It got to the point to where I didn't even leave the room to go upstairs and eat. I had a living area in the basement — it was one big room. I put her hospital bed and her oxygen tank and all the equipment on one side, my bed right next to her bed, and then I had the TV and VCR and stereo on. A lot of times I would put gospel music on.

Both my children are still at home — my son's attending college and my daughter's a sophomore in high school. Up until this point, I have always felt like that this person or that person needed me and I have always been obligated to somebody else, to something else. There comes a time, though, like now, that my health is at the jeopardy point. Before I'll push myself for a goal, and sacrifice my health, I'll put my goals on hold, because right now, my health is more important to me. I'm awfully stressed out right now. I'm just not functioning the way that I feel I should; I think I need some time. I don't feel like I've failed at school and I don't feel that I am a failure in anything that I have set out to accomplish.

Things have never come easy in my family. We were beyond poor — there's no way of describing the level that we were at. It makes you tough, for it's a struggle every day. In the mountains you work. You don't run to malls and you don't have friends in every evening and there's not a party every weekend. You work. You learn responsibility very, very young. You learn how to chop wood — it doesn't matter if you are male or female. It's a job that has to be done and everybody does it. You carry in the water — we'd carry our wash-water in in the evenings for my sister to wash with the next day. We'd start working when we got in from school and it was well after dark when we got finished. We got our baths and we was put to bed. It's hard and it's a struggle, but you survive. It's through that survival that you get the strength. Today's living to some people is very difficult. To me, it's easy. Being cold and being hungry and the struggle — it was all we ever knew so we didn't expect any more. We had what we thought we were supposed to have.

I'm thirty-six and I've learned that even knowing the frightening possibility of failing, you have to try to move on. Somewhere along the line you have to have confidence in yourself. You can't let other people always manipulate you or blame you or tell you you're worthless. You don't have to believe that — you can prove them wrong.

It's that first step that is really the hard one. After the first step, it gets easier and you feel so much better about yourself. There's nothing in this world that any of us could possibly want to do or accomplish in this lifetime that if we want it bad enough and we try hard enough that we can't do it. It's not going to come to us. We have to go to it.

(Evelyn has recently finished Cosmetology school, has passed her exam, and expects to open her own salon in the near future.)

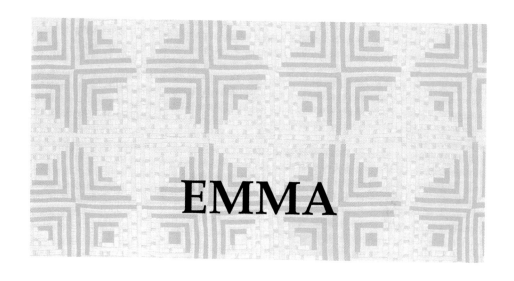

EMMA

I was born in Lee County at a place called Willow Shoals, Kentucky. I grew up nine years in Lee County. When I was born my grandmother was the one that delivered me and all my brothers and sisters. She had thirteen kids of her own. My grandmother was a mid-wife and herbal doctor for the local people — she was my mother's mother and my grandma on Dad's side was also a mid-wife. My grandfather cut hair for people.

My mother had four of us that lived — there were six total, and I'm next to the oldest. We lived on a farm where we grew, raised, dried, and canned almost all of our food. Dad also hunted wild game. We didn't have any type of indoor plumbing or electricity. We had a drilled well where we carried our water from. And, my dad was a farmer, of course. He had mules and plowed — all the breaking of the land. Our farm was part of his mother's farm, which was a total of eighty acres. She gave him fifty of it and he took care of her until her death. When he wasn't farming he worked pumping oil wells in Lee County. He wouldn't get home until after dark and many times I would sit on the porch and watch for the dim glow of his kerosene lantern come into view.

When I first started school I had to walk approximate ten miles and I could only go during the good weather. That's why I didn't anywhere near finish grade school in the one-room schoolhouse at Evelyn, Kentucky. I would get there about lunch time and it just didn't do me any good. But Dad was always the kind that would say, "Study and learn all you can and you can use it at one time or another later on in your life."

When I first started to school I remember being sort of shy and when the teacher would call on me to go to the front of the room to write on the blackboard, I was sort of, I guess you would say, nervous about it. But I overcome that. I remember when I first started I was afraid, never being away except to visit grandparents. We had one teacher for eight grades, and one time I run off and the teacher had to get in her car to catch me — that was when I was real small. Once I got used to it, I wanted to go to school. My older sister went with me all the time I went; then later on my brother went some and then he just dropped out. The school didn't keep up with whether we came or not.

Well, I would read everything I could, including the newspapers, and words I wouldn't know I would look up in the dictionary the best way I could or I would ask Dad. He was a great person to explain everything he could to me. We didn't have very many books, but I still own some books that Dad owned, including a medical book that dated back to 1906.

I had a close relationship with my dad. He taught me how to identify trees, plants, animals, and he even taught me how to go hunting. I went squirrel hunting with him with a twenty-two rifle — a Remington.

After I was about nine years old we moved to Estill County and we went to the same school, but that cut the distance we had to go to about five miles. We walked, and then again, when the weather was bad rainy or in the winter, we just simply couldn't go. I went to school a little bit more than I had been but still yet we lived on a farm and raised most of our food and Dad needed my help. We moved there because there was a tobacco base and Dad thought, well, that would be a better income. My dad was a tenant farmer, so we didn't pay rent. The owners of the farm got one half of what the tobacco would bring. Housing tobacco was probably the hardest job I've ever did because it was heavy and you'd have to raise it straight up into a barn, up into the rafters and someone would be up there who would get a holt of it and hang it. My oldest sister helped some until she moved out, but I stayed and I felt it my responsibility to help. Dad would even pay us so much for doing it. I have one brother, but he's five years younger and by the time he got old enough to help, then dad didn't raise tobacco any more. Mother never helped with tobacco — she one hundred percent stayed in the home and garden — cooking, drying and canning foods for the winter. She repaired clothes, made quilts, picked berries for jams and jellies when in season. Very few items were bought at the local store — cornmeal, flour, sugar, coffee. Dad did a lot of trading for other items so we didn't need a lot of money.

After my oldest sister moved out — there's five years between me and her age — I was Dad's helper. He needed me during the spring — especially when he was really busy planting and then later on in about mid-summer — harvesting all the food. I didn't have time to go to school near like I should but being the "tom boy" that I was, I enjoyed the work and never complained. My time was his. I was his "strong-willed Em," as he called me.

I was raised up like someone two or three times my age, I guess. I was born in 1952 so by the time I was six, it would have been 1958; so we're talking about the early 60's that Dad was farming and I was helping him. I didn't mind working on the farm, it was a way of life. Dad was right there and he encouraged me — I loved working with him. I wouldn't have had it any other way. Where I was born, we didn't even have electric — we used coal oil lamps. Now when we moved into Estill County, there was electric. That was a big change, but we didn't have water in the house. We still had our well outside but it was nice just having a refrigerator. We lived ten years in that same place.

I lived there with my family and then in 1970 I met the man who later fathered my three sons. I met him through other friends. He's from Estill County, and I think he stood out because he had this 1970 Roadrunner and I wasn't ever used to cars. My family didn't have a car — all Dad ever owned, and I got used to riding, was mules. I always wanted a pony but he always said I couldn't have one because it would make the mules too hard for him to control. We never owned any type of vehicle, so when Dad wanted to go to town, he would go down to the local store owner and he would take him wherever he needed to go. I really didn't go into town very often at all until I got way up in my teens. My grandmother on my mother's side lived on the Beattyville Road and I would go up and visit her and stay, oh, a couple of months during the winter time with her. I started school up there in Beattyville. As old as I was and as good as I did, I think I started in like fourth grade. They suggested since I did so well that I should be placed in a higher grade. Still yet, I went for a while and when it come time of the year that Dad needed me I would drop out and go back home and help him.

Oh, I had long-range goals of later on becoming a doctor. Yes, at first I wanted to become a doctor. Then I thought, well, that would be too much so I reduced that to a nurse. I guess I looked ahead and tried to improve whatever situation I was in. That's why a few years ago I wanted to study and go ahead and get my GED. And then I had kids of my own — three sons — and now that they're almost out of high school theirself, I want to go back to school to make something of myself. I'm into my crafts now just because I have a lot of free time at home and I want to make the best use of the time as I can.

Like I said, when I got to be about nineteen, I decided to get away from home. By then Dad didn't tend the tobacco crops so I had more time. I had already traded around somewhere and got me a bike which I rode in my later teen years quite a lot. I was out more on the road and went to visit friends more often and that's when I met my first love. We stayed in Estill County and set up our own housekeeping, which was quite a job for me. I wasn't ever used to it. After my first son was born, my mother helped me a lot with him. It was a big change for someone that had always been an outdoorsy type of person to suddenly find herself with this little baby.

The boys' dad worked in construction as a concrete finisher. He was gone most of the time but he would be back home late in the evening.

Two years later I had my second son; then two years after that I had my third. It's been a plus that they've been close together, I think, because they have growed up together and shared so much. They get along real well and share things even today. I've taught them almost everything that Dad taught me that I can remember. They like it out in the woods and spent quite a lot of time out exploring. When the three boys eventually got old enough to go to school, they went into Estill County. We've lived close to the road and they've rode busses. They went pretty regularly to school. I've made sure that they did.

When my kids first started school, I made a lot of their clothes for them. We could afford to buy clothes since their father was working, but I was more into making everything the way I was used to because Mama made all of ours on the old pedal-type sewing machine.

One time I got a job that was in the sewing factory in Irvine. But I just didn't feel right leaving the boys with their grandparents. So, I quit the job and just simply stayed home and worked on my crafts. That's when I really more and more got into my crafts. I've always wanted to learn how to paint but I didn't do any painting that would amount to anything, but I really couldn't afford to buy paints. I've always collected rocks and arrowheads. I have a bunch of Indian beads, I always called them, but what they really are are petrified weeds that look just like beads. I started collecting those back when I was a teenager. Then I would start drying all the flower's leaves, collecting bark and everything and that's when I started making nature pictures, I call them. I just made them because I liked to work with natural materials and I would give them to friends and family.

We continued to live in Estill County. We were together for eighteen years, I think. I've always been the type of person who looked ahead to improve my situation. Dad always told me it was up to me to make whatever I wanted to make out of myself or make my situation better. I had to work after it, and any fears or anything I've ever had, I've tried to overcome them and meet them head-on.

I think it was about in the mid-80's that I got my GED. I went to take the test to see what areas I was weak on. I had a tutor that come to my home from Lexington — her name was Sister Dorothy. She was a volunteer and she would come, oh, two or three times a week and helped me in all my areas. She told me when she thought I was ready to take the test — she was behind me all the way, any questions I had. I passed immediately with no problems. Mainly she helped me study math — since I read a lot it was easier for me to do all the other subjects but real basic math was all I knew, so

25

algebra and geometry was the toughest. My family was real proud of me when I got it; I think it made the boys want to keep in school.

My mother died in 1975 and my father in 1980. My mother, who left my father, lived in the country and it was stormy the night her house caught on fire. We found out later the house wasn't grounded properly, and she was burnt up in her house that night. And my father, he just got to where he couldn't take care of himself, and me with my small children, I couldn't take care of him. He would take off and I guess you could say he was senile. He wasn't himself; he'd keep going back through the woods, back to his old homeplace — and all over the mountains. He wouldn't stay there with me, so I ended up having to put him in a nursing home because I just simply couldn't take care of him. He didn't live very long after that.

The boys' dad was in a habit of drinking — he drank when I first met him. My dad never did drink. Even though occasionally he made moonshine for extra income, he would say, "It's for selling, not drinking." So I wasn't familiar with anyone who would drink and the problems it would cause. But I felt that I needed to stay because my father was so important to me that I wanted my sons to have theirs. I just stuck it out — I made the best of it.

After my sons got older, that made it much easier to change everything, so we moved to Indiana close to my sister. She said that she would help me in every way she could. I didn't stay up there very long — I think maybe two or three months, and then I moved back. The boys didn't like it in Indiana. They were square ready to come home. They was pleased when I heard an apartment was available with three bedrooms and they was really pleased to get back to their old school and their grandmother and Dad. I had to sign up for all the help I could get — before I moved my sister helped me some but it wasn't enough to pay rent on the trailer I lived in. Then I moved into the public housing at Irvine and even now I still draw public assistance for two of my sons. I've tried to make the crafts as much as I possibly can to cut back on assistance because I don't feel right drawing it.

I've always worked for what I've got. Because of our move to Indiana, my oldest, he dropped out of school and now he's went back to get his GED. The only area he was low in was essay writing. He got a letter just a couple of weeks ago from the lady down there that helped him study and she told him to come in and they'd study like for a week on it then it would be no problem for him to get his GED. He's seventeen. He started working for a person in Estill County that my brother works for at a woodwork shop making outside furniture — he likes making things out of wood, too. My other two boys have stayed in school.

I guess it was about this time that I heard about the New Opportunity School. I couldn't hardly believe it when I first heard about the School. I knew this was perfect for me, and I would do anything I possibly could to get in. After getting the application and getting three people to write recommendations, I knew it was just what I wanted to do. When I got accepted it was a dream come true and I couldn't hardly believe it. I just felt overjoyed. I was a little nervous but looking forward to learning and being placed in a job. I always loved medicine and I wanted to be at the hospital where I could help out there. Through my job there I kind of got an idea of what it would be like to work in a doctor's office. The doctor I worked for there said I did really well. He is a wonderful person.

Besides being placed in my job, which was something I wanted to learn more about, the opportunity to meet more people and be exposed to more things was really important.

My boys were pleased with me coming to the New Opportunity School. Of course they missed me and they was wondering when I was coming home. They stayed with their daddy who, surprisingly, thought it was a good thing for me to do. I was really energized. I felt like, I know I can make it now — I know what's out there. I know how to go about improving myself. I felt like a totally different person, I think. Just being with the other women and finding out you could survive on your own was part of what made me see that I could do it. It helped me a great deal and I made many new friends and we have stayed close. Oh, I would love to come back to the New Opportunity School and go through all that again.

I had started making these little log houses. Then I went to the New Opportunity School workshop on starting a home-based business in crafts and brought some of my log houses and some of the nature pictures I was doing then. We talked about where I could

27

sell my houses. I've sold quite a lot by just simply talking to people about them.

Making these log houses goes back again to my childhood, I guess. Two or three times a year I would go visit the old farm where I was raised and where my grandparents was. That's where I got the idea from — visiting all these old homes that are scattered throughout the mountains up there. The first one I made, I was partially satisfied with it but it wasn't as straight as I wanted it to be — as plumb. It was made of cedar as it's easier to work with.

I started out by going out and just simply cutting my own wood and letting it season and using a pocket knife one hundred percent. Then it took so much time that I had my brother that worked at that wood shop saw me some cedar boards and I could make them a lot faster. It's just basically taking two different lengths of wood, carving the notch and letting that dry where it wouldn't move around and would be straight. Then, just building up and then putting the rafters on — then the roof, windows, doors, porches — whatever. Just like a real house.

Then I started making the chimneys out of stone. I wanted them to look more real. I had started out using only cedar blocks for the chimneys. Then I wanted to make them more realistic looking so I made the main base of cardboard, built that out of whatever I wanted and simply covered it with creek gravel that I went out and found. I would glue each little rock on.

Then it just come to me to start making other things — little trees and fences. I guess it comes from being familiar with the country way of life. Someone wanted a barn with a sheep or something in it and I thought about making a chicken to sit up on the gate of the barn. That's the first time that had crossed my head. I get all these ideas, you know, they just pop in my head. Then I use whatever is available to me. People like the little extras — the chairs, people, animals, flowers — the accessories make the houses. The ones that are most popular are the small ones with dog trots or the two-story ones. Mainly the ones with people and animals and all sells best. It makes the houses look more real.

I've had some other changes in my life recently. Now I'm living at a church camp as care-taker — I've been there six or seven months now. I like it out in the country but I mainly moved because of my sons. They're exposed to a different life in government housing than out in the country. I was anxious to find a place where they could have their space, and this place is in walking distance to their grandmother's. I found out about this place through friends; they told me the people that was living there was moving and it was mine if I wanted it. I take phone messages and generally keep up the place, which includes mowing the yards. We get to live in the house for taking care of it. When we moved there all the inside of the house needed to be re-done. I just mainly put up dry wall, hung some doors and painted — built closets with the help of my family. We are real happy with it. It was an old house and two or three years ago some person came up to the church and volunteered his time and laid sandstone around the outside of the house. It's a beautiful home outside and now it is inside, since I've pretty well gotten my work on it complete.

We've been real happy living out in the country again. The boys still go to their same school, just ride the bus. They kept their same friends and everything. I had bought an old car just before we moved out to the country — it's necessary up there.

Between my job of taking care of the camp and seeing that it is looking nice and remodeling the house, I don't have a whole lot of time for my crafts, but I hope to continue and expand some. Later on I would like to go back to school. Soon my two boys that are in high school will be finishing and then I will have time for myself. My sons are my main responsibility now and I want to do everything I possibly can for them. That's the way I was taught growing up. But I can see a time coming when I can go back to school and become a nurse. I still have that interest, and I think that's where I'm strongest. I could even work in surgery. I've been in a few situations where people's got hurt and I can jump in and take care of them without even thinking — I do it automatically — I don't mind the sight of blood. Going back a few years before my youngest son was born, their father was into drinking quite a lot and he got into a fight with another person and was stabbed in the chest. I took care of him and kept him alive without any training. First I called the ambulance then I kept him awake and applied pressure to the wound. It was bleeding pretty bad since it was the main artery. We lived about eight miles out in the country and it takes awhile for the ambulance to get there but I kept him alive — I was too busy to be scared. He was in the hospital one solid month because he had to have open heart surgery.

I feel good about my future. I know if I try, I can make it. Anything I have a fear of or don't know about, I try to overcome it. It's like some people are afraid of snakes. But I've caught snakes before — just secure the head where it can't bite you and there's no problem.

But my crafts — I'll still keep making them — that's just a natural part of me, I guess. Recently I have started making wooden snakes. I don't know what it will be after the snakes. I guess it just hasn't come to me yet.

(Emma is still making crafts and has expanded her sales to include craft fairs. She no longer lives and works at the church camp as all her sons are now away from home. One son is currently a student at Berea College.)

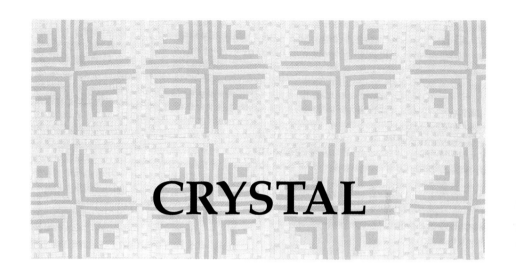

CRYSTAL

I grew up in a little place, Sand Gap. I have three brothers and six sisters, all but two are younger than I am. We grew up very rough because both of our parents were alcoholics. When I was very small, two or three years old, my mother didn't drink near as much, but then I had a little sister that died. She was three months old when she died and after that my mother just went downhill, and she has been drunk ever since. Most of the rest of my life I never knew her any way except drunk. My mother is still alive and still lives in Sand Gap.

My father died four years ago. He drank himself to death. He drank just enough to stop his heart. He was tired of living. He had cancer and they'd operated and operated and they told him that they'd got it all, but it kept coming back and he just couldn't take anymore. But he had drank himself to death too — he'd drank enough during that weekend he died to just stop his heart.

Mother lives by herself now and is doing better than I've ever known her to do — she is what's known as a "dry drunk." Not everybody knows what that means. A "dry drunk" is an alcoholic that all of a sudden stops drinking but they haven't been to AA meetings and worked the twelve steps of AA. So, physically they're not drinking, but mentally their mind is still just as drunk as if they were drunk on alcohol.

Growing up as a child of alcoholic parents, my grandmother

31

was about the only person in my life that I had to hang on to. Although she wasn't that active in our life, we knew that she was there close and that when it came to safety that we had a place to go to for a little while without ever telling her what was really going on.

We would be left alone for days by ourselves with me to take care of the children, and we never knew where our parents was at or when they was coming back. We never knew what we was going to have to eat. Most of the times it was cornbread and milk. My older brother would go milk the cow and we would have a glass of milk and green onions, as we could go out on the creek bank and pull up the green onions that grows there. If things got bad enough I would take the children and go to my grandmother's and she would give them something to eat then I would bring them back home.

I first started looking after the rest of the children when I was eight. I started in school at the elementary school the year that they built it, but it really got bad for me when I was in the sixth grade. I wasn't in school very much because I had to take care of the little ones in the afternoon when my mother worked. But she worked to support their drinking habit. We didn't profit from it any at all. My father worked at plumbing around and about, but he drank. We just didn't have anything. Our house was like an open bar. The whole community knew that that was the place to go to drink. Everybody came there. It was just an open public bar was what it was.

I would go to school and I worked in the lunchroom from ten of the morning until one-thirty in the afternoon in order to pay for the kids' lunches at school. Then at one-thirty my mother would come and pick me up from school. She would meet me outside and take me home and I would watch the little ones at home while she left and went to work.

All the school I got was from eight thirty to ten in the morning. My teacher knew the situation of my parents' drinking, so she permitted them to come and pick me up and take me home. I was looking after my three sisters that hadn't even started school, and then I watched the others after they got in from school. My teacher would make out my work assignments that the other students would do through the day and I would take them home with me. In between times when there was nobody there but just me and the kids, when I would get them quiet and had them fed, then I could work on my homework. The biggest part of the time I went and sat up on top of the garage. We had a big tree there that covered the top of the garage with limbs and I would get on top of the garage and sit there and do my homework.

My daddy was very, very strict about us bringing homework home — that was strictly a no-no — you just did not do that. Homework was something you did at school. He thought it was the teacher's job to learn you at school because when you got home you had work to do — you did not have time to do homework from school.

I LOVED school. I can remember when I got in the eighth grade we had a dance. They called it decorating the maypole. I was chosen to be in that dance and I didn't want to be because I didn't have anything decent to wear. But my teacher had a sister that was the same age and grade as I was and she loaned me one of her dresses to wear to do that dance. It really didn't make any difference because there was never anybody from home there to watch any of it anyway — just like there was never anybody there when we graduated. We graduated and that was it.

I got real attached to my teacher because I had her in the sixth, seventh and eighth grade. Ever time I moved up a year she moved up a year. When I got ready to graduate, I cried. Oh, I didn't want to graduate; I didn't want to leave that school and leave her because I was leaving the only decent thing there was in my life. I begged her to fail me so I wouldn't have to leave that school and she kept telling me, "Crystal, I cannot do that. I can't fail you. Your grades are too good. I have to pass you on." I graduated and I remember filling out all my papers for high school — the classes I was going to take. That didn't do me any good anyway because I graduated in May and in June I got married.

If I had gone on to high school, I would have been leaving early in the morning on the school bus and coming back late in the afternoon. My mother didn't like that — she was more agreeable for me to get married. You know, my mother worked of the night, so the cooking, the cleaning, and taking care of the kids — getting them up and ready for school the next morning and seeing that they had something to eat for breakfast — that was all my responsibility.

We never had anybody to tell us anything about growing up — what to expect, what not to expect. One thing that I can remember that terrified me was when I turned twelve and a half years old and started my period. Me and my sister had walked to Annville and back. I can remember that I had blood all over me and I did not know where it came from. She laughed at me, my older sister did. She thought that was the funniest thing that ever was — because I was terrified. I thought I was dying, I literally did. She never would tell me what was wrong. I knew that it wasn't something you would go and say anything about to your mother. That was just out of the question. My sister laughed and laughed and laughed for hours and I cried. Finally, she did give me one of her pads to use. She said, "Here — use this and it'll take care of it." When I got to school the next day I went to my teacher and asked her what was wrong with me and she told me. The next day she called the whole class together and took us girls off to ourselves and explained what was happening to us. There was others that didn't know either — but that was terrifying to me.

My older sister never had to help out at home because she was seeing whoever she could see just to be away from home. She had already stopped school and she had gotten involved with a married man. I can remember many, many times that this man's wife came to the house and asked where her husband and my sister was at because she knew that he was seeing her.

My parents knew that I was dependable and never gave them any problems at all. My grandmother had implanted in me that regardless of what my parents did, what they said, how they acted, it didn't make any difference — still, in God's eyes they were my parents and I was to obey what they said. At that time my sister and I was going to church with her. It was just a little church right outside the house. I can remember her saying to me so many times, "Honor thy mother and father for our days may be shortened upon this earth." And I guess I thought if I ever said anything back to them that God was just going to strike me down right where I was standing. I can't remember ever saying anything back to my mother and father. Even to this day I just can't do that. I can't ever remember getting spanked for doing anything wrong or saying anything back, but I can remember my brothers and sisters doing it often and although my mother never whipped one of my brothers and sisters, my daddy always did.

I can remember so many times going and hiding when he was whipping one of us, or coming out and trying to get him to whip me instead to get him to stop beating on them. He wouldn't. He just kept beating and beating and I never could understand why. Even going to church as much as I did, it made me stop believing in God all together. I would go to church, I would try to do everything I was suppose to do. I can remember one of the girls at church talked me into letting her paint my fingernails and I was so scared because I knew that that was wrong — people who went to church didn't polish their fingernails and I worked for days trying to get that stuff off my fingers. I prayed so hard to God to forgive me for letting her put that stuff on my fingers. And I would pray for Him just to take my parents out of my life and to tell me what I was doing wrong that was making them do these things. I can remember praying so hard when I was in church that if He couldn't make them stop — to just let me die. Just to let me die. But He would never even do that either. After that, I lost all confidence in Him, I guess. My grandmother always told me, "Crystal, regardless of what happens, God always looks after little children. He never lets them get hurt." But then, He wasn't — He wasn't looking after us. He let us all get hurt by what these grown people were doing.

My brothers and sisters and I don't talk about it. Everybody just kind of went their separate ways. A lot of their actions come from those days. I would like to see them be able to work through it and change their ways. My youngest brother, he's been in the pen most of his life and he likes it there. That is his home. That is the only place he has ever felt safe. It is very sad, but it is easy for me to see because he was abused really bad when he was little. All he can ever remember is hearing his daddy tell him that he hated him. And he never knew why — he just knew that he hated him. Bobby was constantly getting beat for something. He could do nothing right, regardless. It seemed just to breathe, the child did wrong.

I can remember when my oldest brother, Jimmy, was twelve

or thirteen he went to Annville one day to his friend's house. Daddy had it in his head that this friend was no good for Jimmy to be around, but Jimmy sneaked off and went anyway. Well, when Daddy found out that was where he was at, he went after him. He brought him back and went out and cut a stick. He beat Jimmy till he couldn't stand. I can remember begging him to quit, to leave him alone for awhile, to whip me if he needed to whip somebody else for awhile. He just kept beating and beating and beating until the blood was running out of Jimmy's back, down his arms and his legs until finally he got tired and quit. I washed Jimmy off and put salve on his places. He stayed in the bed and out of school for a week because he wasn't able to get up.

I met Joe when I was in the eighth grade. I was thirteen. He would come by the house and he drank with my mother and daddy. He was nine years older than me. He had stopped school and his family didn't go very far in school either. It seemed like when things would go wrong and nobody else was there, from somewhere he would always show up. I remember one time all the lights went out and we were completely in the dark and it was storming and all the fuses had blown in the house. He took us and got some fuses and put them back in and got the lights back on. I got to talking to him and I guess I just got real attached to him. We never went anywhere — we'd just sit in his car. After I got the kids into bed, I'd sit in the car in front of the house and talk to him for awhile.

I was going with him for four months before my mother and daddy even knew it. That is odd for somebody's daughter to be going with somebody and seeing them right there in the house together and them not even know you are going together. They liked him because he drank with them. As long as somebody drank with them it was okay. It was people who didn't drink that was the "outside people," and they wasn't welcome.

Joe worked through the day and then he would drink of the evening. It didn't seem to bother me because he drank, maybe because I wasn't that involved in it. It gave me a little peace — as long as I could talk to him, then I was out and away from them.

When Joe and I got married we moved out and I can remember my daddy saying that he hated to lose me, but I knew that the only reason he hated to lose me was because I would not be there to do all of that work for them anymore. That was the only reason. My mother and my brother signed the papers to let me get married. You know, they had to do that because I was thirteen. It was a welcoming relief just to get away, but I hated to leave my brothers and sisters there. It made them cry that I couldn't take them with me — that I was going to have to leave them there and that I couldn't protect them anymore.

In a very short time, I found myself pregnant and it was really odd because I never even knew what that was. When my mother was pregnant I never knew what the word meant, I just knew that there was a new baby on the way and we would be took to my grandmother's till the midwife came. We were always told that she brought the baby when she came — that's all we knew. When we were brought back home there was a new baby there to take care of. I felt so stupid being married and pregnant and here I was, thirteen, and I didn't know the first thing about what being pregnant was. Joe told me what it meant to be pregnant — that I was going to have a baby. I felt that at least I would have somebody to love and take care of again.

We had moved into the house with his mother for a few months, then we moved down to Tyner. When I had April I was fourteen years old. I went to the hospital to have her but I never went to the doctor until I was nine months pregnant because I didn't know I was suppose to go to the doctor. I didn't know the first thing that was happening. When I was getting ready to go into labor I just knew that I felt bad. My back hurt me all night long one night and when I got up the next morning. We were at Joe's mother's and still my back was killing me. I didn't know what was happening. She saw me setting on the bed holding my back and she asked me if I was okay. I said I was okay but that my back was hurting me real bad. She asked me how long it had been hurting and I said, "All night," and she explained to me that I was getting ready to have that baby. So Joe took me to the hospital. I had no earthly idea where this baby was coming from or what was going to happen to me and I was just terrified.

I can remember the nurses saying to me, "You can't have a baby, you're just a child yourself." I was getting so mad at the nurses for saying that to me. I wanted to scream at them that they didn't know what they was talking about — that I had never been a child so don't tell me now that I'm a child and that I can't have this baby.

April was born in November and in December of the following year I had my second child, Tony. There was a very short span until I was pregnant again. I never went to the hospital until eight and nine months. I never went back for my six-weeks checkups unless my kids got sick and my kids were never sick enough to have to be taken to the hospital or to the doctor or anything.

I had a child when I was fourteen and one when I was fifteen. I had a miscarriage when I was sixteen. I had another child when I was seventeen, one when I was eighteen and one when I was nineteen. So there at one time I had four of them in bottles and diapers at one time. Actually, at the time, it was no problem. I had been used to that all my life and it was like I was just a child raising little kids all over again. I never felt like a woman because that was something I never wanted to be. To be a woman meant that I was going to act like all these other women that had been in my life — to drink and do the things that they done. I would never allow myself to be that way.

During this time I saw my grandmother a little bit but not very much. She was a smart woman who had had fourteen kids. I would see her enough that she would tell me little things — little "wives tales" from the old-time people — like running the babies through horse collars. She would do that when something happened to one of them. I don't know why, but she would tell me to run it through a horse collar and it took care of whatever was wrong with the baby. She would make worm candy and get the kids to eat it. Worm candy is green as grass. She made it out of a weed that she grew out of her yard. It was suppose to help them get rid of worms. They would eat green apples and green apples was suppose to cause kids to get worms, but if they ate that candy, it would take care of it. When the little ones would laugh in their sleep that means they've got hives and to take care of that they needed some catnip tea to help them sleep at night. She would fix that for them and let them drink it in their bottle and that would take care of it. I am real proud of her because there were times that I don't know what we would have done if it hadn't been for her. You know my daddy was her pride and joy. He was her first child, and she never wanted to accept what he was. He always tried to keep that hid from her. They didn't like for me to go around her much because they knew if she wanted to know something about him that I would tell her and they didn't like that.

So, Joe and I were living this side of Tyner and when April first started school and had been going about two months, we moved here to Annville. We've been here eighteen years in the same house and Joe's had the same job farming for Mr. Thomas.

I stayed home with my kids. I always told myself that if I ever got married that I would see to it, regardless what I had to do, that my kids was not done the way we were done. They would not be left alone. I would always be there for them, regardless. I never took them anywhere and left them. They were always with me. One or two of them stayed all night with Joe's mother once in a while, but that's the only place they ever stayed. I never even thought about working anywhere because my place was at home, taking care of my kids and my husband. That was the only thing I was for.

If it hadn't been for my kids I don't know how I would ever got along. Somewhere along the line, standards just stuck with me all these years. It wasn't until Penny started high school that I even considered going out of the house and trying to work. She started high school and all of a sudden I felt like I didn't have anything in life, you know. My kids didn't need me anymore and I didn't have any reason for anything anymore. It was like lightning came down and struck me one day and I got scared. I didn't know what I was going to do because I didn't have anyone to take care of anymore, nobody that needed me twenty-four hours a day. I realized, too, that I didn't have any education any further than the eighth grade, and very little up to the eighth grade. I didn't know the first thing about going out and getting a job — how to go about it, where to go or what to say to people — anything. I never got my driver's license until I'd been married for twelve years.

My niece worked through the summer at the Mt. Vernon Hospital and she asked me why I didn't work there. I said, "Because I had never worked anywhere." But she said, "You can get on up there." I said, "How?" She said, "They're going to have another program in two months where you go up and take a week's train-

39

ing and after that they hire you as a nurse assistant, which is taking care of the patients in the hospital." At this time, my daughter, April, was out of high school also. I was scared to death so I talked to April and we both decided we'd take this course.

Well, April came out top in her class, which didn't surprise me because she had done well in high school, but what did surprise me was when I came out second. I couldn't believe I had done that. Two weeks later they called us and we were both hired. We worked different shifts and different sides of the hospital — we never worked together while we were there. I was part-time for a year then I went to full-time for four years. But, before I decided to go to work, I was going through a period that even today I don't know what it was. I just know that things was changing for me, especially for me to think about working.

I hadn't been working for very long before I had to go into the hospital for surgery and after I had surgery it seemed like every thing in my life went haywire. There wasn't anything I could control anymore. I went in for a hysterectomy and my doctor had explained to me that because of my age — I was only thirty-four — big changes would be in my life because it was going to throw me into the "change" real early. Yet, he didn't tell me what to expect. When I came home from the hospital I didn't want anything to eat. I had no appetite whatsoever. While I was in there, I ate jello and crackers and when I come home that's what I ate. I was off six weeks from work and during that time all I ate was jello and crackers — and I was having to force myself to eat that.

When I went back for my six-weeks check-up I told my doctor that all I was eating was jello and crackers and drinking grape-fruit juice. I told him, I am walking myself to death and I want to know what's causing it. I was walking fifteen to eighteen miles a day. I had more energy than I knew what to do with.

I was taking Liberax, which is a pill for gas on your stomach. I had been on those because I had had gallbladder surgery before. That's all I was taking, and I asked him if that was what was doing it and he said, "They don't have anything to do with it." I said, "Then what is wrong?" He said, "Right now I don't know, but I know you can't keep this up." I said, "I know I can't either. I am wearing myself out. I am walking myself to death and I can't stop

40

it."

After six weeks, I started back to work and I found myself walking circles around everybody in the hospital. I couldn't be still. I wasn't eating lunch or supper. When meal times come, I would go walking through town for an hour. Any time they needed someone to work overtime, I would work overtime and when they needed someone to double-shift, I would double-shift. Then I would come home and I would walk and walk and walk, and when I wasn't walking I was running. I would come home and fix meals for the kids and Joe, then I would go out and walk some more. When I wasn't doing that I would get somebody to play badminton with me and after that I would walk some more. I don't know where the energy was coming from. After that I would get so tired, yet I couldn't set down. I lost sixty-eight pounds.

I couldn't eat. If I ate, I couldn't stomach the thought of eating anything but jello, crackers, and grapefruit juice. And I was having to force myself to do that and I knew at that time something was going on. The people around the hospital kept telling me, "Crystal, you have got to do something about this. Something is going to happen to your body if you don't." I couldn't figure out why these people were so worried about me because I felt better than I had ever felt in my life. The cooks at the hospital tried to stop me from getting jello and crackers — they tried to make me eat other stuff. But when I would eat other stuff, I would end up in the ER. The pain was that severe because my stomach had shrunk and it couldn't handle food anymore.

I just kept losing weight and exercising. I found that I couldn't sleep anymore. My fingernails were slitting and cracking off. My hair was falling out. My skin was turning. I went back to my doctor and asked him, "What is going on with me? Why are all these things happening?" Still, he told me, "I don't know," but he said, "It is going to put you in the hospital."

During that time he set me up an appointment to see Jill at Comp Care in McKee. She had only been there two weeks when he set me up an appointment with her and I went out there and talked to her. I can remember getting real angry with her the first time I ever met her and I asked her point blank, "Here you are, probably twenty something years old and I am thirty-four. What do you think

41

you can tell me that I don't already know?" I said, "I do want you to know one thing, regardless of what you think, or the doctor may think, I am not crazy." I had got real defensive when I found out where I was going to go.

She said, "I never said you was crazy."

I said, "No, but they sent me here to this crazy trailer," which is what it was called.

She asked me after that, "Crystal, have you ever been sexually abused?"

I said, point-blank, "NO," and she dropped it — never asked me anymore.

Well, we talked and talked. She would set up appointments twice a week and I would go to see her because it was my duty to go to see her. After awhile it was not my duty anymore — it was because I wanted to.

I was still working. Jill knew my dream was to go to school; she knew my background. She said to me, "Why don't you go to school?"

And I said, "Because I can't. At my age? You don't go back to high school at my age."

She said, "Crystal, you don't have to go back to high school. Take your GED."

I said, "WHAT is a GED?"

She said, "You can take a test and see if you pass out of high school."

I said, "Jill, I can't do that. I never went any farther than the eighth grade. I can't do that."

She said, "Yes, you can. I will help you do that."

So, we went to the Family Life Center where they do the testing for the GED and where they let you have the books. It is operated by the Christian Appalachian Project. I had two sisters who was going to go with me, so here we all three went — and they were tickled to death down there that they had three from the same family that wanted to get their GED. So they worked with us. We just went when we felt the need. My other two sisters, neither of them worked, so they could go down there full-time or whenever they wanted to. Both of them got their GEDs, one of them before I did. I was trying to work and find time to study for my GED and take care of my family all at the same time so mine took longer. When I run into problems, like with this algebra stuff, it liked to have drove me crazy. It was like a foreign language to me. I had never even seen an algebra problem, much less know how to work one.

Jill kept encouraging me and helping me with my algebra and a woman named Wendy was also helping me with my algebra. Finally, I decided I was ready to go try for my GED. They set me up an appointment over at Eastern Kentucky University. I went over and took it and I lacked only two points passing my test. They told me I didn't have to take all of it, just pick one subject because I only lacked two points.

Since I had passed everything except the algebra I studied the algebra. Jill helped me a lot when I went in for my sessions with her — sometimes we would just set there and work on the algebra. With Jill and Wendy helping me, when I went back I passed. That was three years ago.

At that time, I was still losing weight and Jill was getting real, real concerned about me. She was a four-year RN besides being a therapist so she knew something was wrong. She also figured out what was wrong with me. She told me that I had anorexia.

I said, "What is anorexia?"

She said, "It is an eating disorder you've got and that is why you aren't eating and why you are loosing all this weight. You cannot go on this way — you are killing yourself."

I had lost seventy-eight pounds by that time and I said, "Why didn't my doctor tell me what was wrong with me?" She said, "These doctors here don't know enough about eating disorders to know how to diagnose what's wrong with you."

I figured out that when I didn't eat that things were crazy. My thinking was distorted. I was having nightmares in the day time. My whole house turned into a nightmare and the people that were there weren't the people who lived there — they were monsters that were appearing in the day time. I would find myself sitting in the middle of my bed screaming that monsters were coming over the foot of the bed after me.

With Jill's help we worked very closely on nothing but my eating disorder until we got it somewhat under control. She had me

43

making lists of what all I would eat for her. She knew me enough to know that if I promised her, then I would eat what was on my list. I didn't have to go in the hospital, but I didn't gain any of my weight back. I went down to one hundred and ten pounds and I pretty much stayed there. It took a year and a half until I could eat what you would say was a normal meal. My stomach had shrunk so much until it was making me sick. I had to deal with that and was trying to work and take care of my family and get my GED — all of that together was about more than I could handle.

During that time we worked on my eating and Jill would talk to me about different things. One thing she showed me was this pamphlet about the New Opportunity School at Berea College. It was hanging up in her office — posted up there. She asked me why I didn't go to it.

I said, "I can't go to that." She said, "Why not?" I said, "I can't." She said, "It's just over at Berea College." I said, "I still can't — I am working, I've got the kids. I can't." She said, "Well, at least think about it."

She gave me the pamphlet and I took it and thought about it a lot. The more I thought, the more I told myself I couldn't go. The more I told her I couldn't go, the more she would encourage me to write for the information and at least read it and then decide. So I did. I got the information. I filled out the application. I kept telling myself, "Well, I am going to fill it out and send it back but nothing's going to come out of it so I won't worry about nothing."

Then the papers came back to me telling me I was accepted for the New Opportunity School, and then I got scared. I was scared to death. I wanted to back out. I was terrified at what I had done. I had wrote for this information, got accepted and what had I done? It was like a bomb had fell down out of the sky and hit me.

I told her, "Jill, now what am I going to do? Jane wrote and told me I was accepted, now what am I going to do?"

She said, "Go to it. Crystal, it is only for three weeks. You will only have to go over there and stay for three weeks."

I said, "No, I can't do that. You know I can't do that."

"Well, why not?" she said.

I said, "I've got the kids at home. Joe is at home. I've got to watch after them, and cook for them, and keep house. Who is going to do that if I am not there?"

She said, "Crystal, how old are your kids? How old? Tell me, how old is Penny?"

I said, "She is fifteen."

Jill said, "Is that a child?"

I said, "NO."

She said, "When you were fifteen where were you at?"

I said, "I had three kids."

She said, "What do you think is going to happen if you are not there for three weeks?"

I said, "I don't know — the house will fall down I guess. I've never NOT been there."

She said, "Well, don't you think it is about time you did something for yourself?"

I said, "Jill, I have never done anything for myself. You don't know what you are asking."

Jill said, "Yes, I do." She told me time after time: "Crystal, if you only had half the confidence in you that I have in you, you could do anything that you want to do in life."

When I was feeling real sure that I was going to go to the School, things would get crazy — all the nightmares were still going on. As far along in therapy as I was, we was working through things in my childhood and it was making me re-live all that over and it made things crazy in my life.

Also, I was terrified of not being able to see Jill during that three weeks. I was seeing her at that time six days a week of my own accord. We had a special kind of relationship which wasn't like a doctor-patient. At least it wasn't for me. It had grown so close, our relationship, that I had been able to have confidence in her that I haven't been able to have in anybody. I just felt free and safe with her to say whatever I had to say. For me to be away from her for that three weeks was terrifying.

Well, I went to the School and I never wanted to go home. Being in school was just where I was meant to be.

I saw Jill on Friday nights. I had gotten permission to leave the School to go to my ACA meetings because they were very important to me. I go to ACA groups — which is Adult Children of Alcoholics, and now I'm very active in ANON. That is a support

45

group for spouses or children or anybody that has any kind of abuse in their background. It doesn't even have to be alcohol. It can be drugs. It can be sexual abuse. It can be just growing up with or having somebody that you care about that drinks. I have never drank and I've never had any desire to, even though my husband does. Anyway, I was very scared but Jill kept up with me by phone. She knew how scared I was and she told me before I went that she would keep in contact with me over the phone. I called her quite a bit and twice she even came over to see me. Once she came up to see my room where I was staying. To this day, she is the most special person in my life, mostly as a friend now — not as a therapist.

So, I came to the New Opportunity School and my family didn't like it at all. It was taking me away from them and they were seeing all those things that I wasn't going to be able to do for them for three weeks. It was making me feel real bad for leaving them. I cried the whole week before I left because I was going to leave them. Right up until that day before I was to come I was about to back out and not show up — the guilt had built that much.

So I told myself, "Alright, I am going to do it. This one time, I am going to do it for myself. If I don't, everything will stay just like it is. This opportunity will never come again if I don't take it. So, I am going."

I packed my stuff. I said, "You all can do the best you can do for the next three weeks. The house won't fall down. You won't go hungry. There is a washer in there, you all know how to use it. I will be back in three weeks." I said, "One thing I ask of you while I am gone — you don't write me, you don't call me — this three weeks is mine. I have give you all my whole life; this three weeks is mine to do what I want to do with."

We didn't have any contact at all and when I got back they were real distant to me. Everybody was afraid because I had changed so much during that time. I could see that in myself, but I didn't realize that other people could see that also. I was real hurt that they were distant to me, that they wouldn't talk to me, wouldn't have any thing to do with me at all. It was like this stranger had come in, put her stuff up, and had come here to live. And, I was real hurt by that. They didn't understand why I would do this — why I would leave them for three weeks. I had never done that before. It just wasn't me. They had already seen so many different changes. They didn't know what to expect next. I can realize how scared they was, but, I didn't know what to do about it. When I was at the School the most helpful thing that happened to me was finding confidence in people that I had never known. Just to be able to be with grown people for three weeks was helpful because the only grown people I had ever been with in my life was my people and Joe's people. Me and him. Outside of that, the rest of the world didn't exist. I didn't have any friends or any other women I could talk to. It was real strange to me to be able to be at the New Opportunity School for Women and nobody be there but women. I felt totally comfortable where nobody was at but women.

It helped to have another woman as a roommate to talk to and be close to. The first night I didn't have a roommate. I was by myself and I felt so at peace. I can remember when my roommate didn't show up I felt relief because I was worried about what that person was like and if she was going to accept me. I was that down on myself that when she didn't show up, I was relieved. When I learned she was coming the next day, I was on pins and needles waiting for her to come. Meanwhile, I was getting acquainted with the other women.

I found it really strange that the more we talked, it seemed like we all had so much in common. I felt like, "Hey, I am not the only one out there that has these problems." Everybody else was saying, "Hey, I do, too, but in different ways." It seemed like everything we did hit home with me. All the things that the teacher talked about in the Appalachian Literature class was like he came inside myself and was talking about me. Sometimes I would even take it personally and it would make me hurt, but I never said anything. Here I was, ashamed of who I was and where I come from and here he is teaching classes on the same people from the same background — people that I was ashamed of being part of. After awhile, I felt proud — and not ashamed of where I come from.

The self-esteem classes were excellent, just excellent. The other women and I just didn't have any self-esteem. I am not sure we had ever had any. I didn't know what the word meant. But the more the counselor worked with us you could just see the confidence build in ourself. It was amazing to see the changes in all of us from the day we walked in and three weeks later. These are not the same women that came in here three weeks ago — what happened to them?

I loved being on campus. For the first time in my life I got to feel and act free of responsibilities at home. I hated the fact that I didn't want to go back home and I cried many times over that. I was so guilty over not wanting to go back home but I wanted to stay at the School. The day we had to leave and go back home, I cried three hours before I ever could leave and go home. I just walked around the campus three hours before I had the nerve to go home.

After the New Opportunity School was over, I went back to work. And I kept changing. It was like a whole new world had opened up. At this time, it was either my family understand — or they don't. Whatever is happening to me, I can't stop it.

That was February. That next summer, Eastern Kentucky University offered a sociology class in McKee. I took it and come out with an A. That kind of boosted my confidence that I could go to school. After Sociology, I signed up for and took two more classes that fall. I took those of a night while I was working of a day. I would leave work and go to Eastern on Monday and Wednesday nights. I would go over there on Saturdays also. I made good grades again. I got an A on one and a B on one.

I took my ACT before I started in at Eastern. Then the next January I quit my job. That summer I started off taking four classes but I ended up taking three. I was lucky enough to get them all off-campus this time.

Even going to school just the time that I'm going is hard because my life is in such a mess right now at home. It really makes it hard about concentrating but I'm passing my classes. I keep a journal all the time and write down constantly everyday what's going on, and my feelings, and my thoughts, and that really helps.

I have changed even more than I had realized. I find that I am not happy at home any more because I feel like I don't have anything there any more. I have grown completely away from that other person I used to be. That other person never existed. I don't know who she was or where she came from. I'm glad that person is gone and she can't never return. I'm beginning to like the person

48

I'm becoming a lot more and it makes me very sad that my family can't accept this new person. They work so hard against me to get that old person back, yet, I keep telling them that that person is gone and she can't ever return.

Joe has told me time and time again that he wants the old Crystal back. He can't accept this new one. That makes me very sad because the more I change I'm growing more away from him. I know my marriage is ending and I can't stop it. It's got to the point that Joe is drinking more and more and it brings back too many memories of the past. He's blaming me for his drinking because of who I am now. My family, all of them — since I've started changing — say I'm just an outsider to all of them. I am not accepted by any of them. My children don't talk about who I am now. They're just about as distant as Joe is because they don't understand.

They like me going to school but they can't understand how and why I have to be away from them so much. I now have three grandchildren. My oldest child, April, finished high school and then after she got out of high school she got married. She was married a year and she decided she was going to go to college, so she started taking some off-campus classes and then she ended up signing up over at Eastern. She's still going. She lacks two semesters being a four-year RN now. She has two little boys, and I am very proud of her.

My next daughter quit when she was in the twelfth grade. She says she's thinking about getting her GED, but she never went back and done it. She just stays home with her little boy.

Then there's Johnny. He quit when he was in the twelfth grade. He lacked six months graduating and he had a lot of trouble with the bus driver and that caused him to quit. They told him he could pass his GED test with flying colors but he's never done it.

Robert is at home now. He graduated out of high school and is helping his Daddy work around the farm here. He's not married.

And, Penny, she's still in high school. She's sixteen and a junior this year with good grades and taking honors courses. As for others, I've always been there and they expect me to always be there. Here I am at this stage and trying to get through to them: YOU ARE YOUNG ADULTS AND YOU HAVE TO LOOK AFTER YOURSELVES. They look at me like, "You don't love me anymore; you're making me do all these things; why are you not willing to do them anymore?"

It makes me feel bad that they feel this way. They make me feel guilty and it really hurts me. I cry a lot over my marriage ending and think, "Why? Why is it happening?" Joe won't talk to anyone about it. He don't want to understand and he's told me time and time again that, "I'm not changing for anybody. I am just like I am. Take it or leave it, I am just like I am. I won't ever be any different."

Well, I didn't think I'd be any different either. I didn't do it intentionally; it just happened. It makes me sad because I know if he'd give it a chance, it would happen for him too. Maybe that scares him, because it scared me not knowing where I was going. It also scares me that somewhere across that time that together we had become one person. I never was a person until now. I never even existed. Before, my thoughts were his thoughts and my actions were his actions. I can see that now where I couldn't before.

But right now, it's just like a never-ending world of experiences. I'm scared, but more confident than what I was. I've never had to take care of me. I've always had someone else to take care of but never me. That scares me, but I know that it won't stop me.

The growing has begun and there's no stopping it. Whether I like it or not I can't stop it so I'm just going with the flow and see where I'll land. Right now I don't know what my future is going to be. There's so many exciting things happening; yet, some are sad. I don't know where it's going to end up. Just knowing that I had the chance to go to the New Opportunity School made a world of difference because of the things I got to see while I was there. I had never seen an art museum before in my life and never dreamed of being able to. When things get really hard, I remember Alex Haley saying to us, "If you don't try, you can't ever get anywhere. You've got to have that confidence!!" I am so thankful that the New Opportunity School came into my life because that has given me a sense of direction. I wouldn't be the healthy person that I am now without the School and therapy.

When I see people down on themselves and think they can't do anything at all, that they can't even start, I try to talk to them.

I say, "Hey, you can. If I can, anybody can!"

50

(Crystal is currently working in the Social Work Department of a local hospital. She and Joe have divorced and she is now living in her own new house.)

KATIE

I don't remember much of my early life. It's sort of like a block in my mind. I know I was born at Berea Hospital and my family lived about six miles away. I was number ten of eleven children. A very stern, but loving, mother took care of the family. Daddy took care of us financially but Mama did what you call "the raising." I mean, what she said went.

At the time I was born, Daddy worked at the Blue Grass Ordinance in Richmond, Kentucky, making sixty-nine cents an hour. I'll never forget that because he's told me several times. And he's been a part-time farmer, a full-time farmer, and he worked at Eastern Kentucky University almost nine years as grounds keeper for Robert R. Martin at the president's house. He did a real good job up there. He kept that place real neat, and he got along real well with the president and his wife, and especially the cook who fixed his breakfast every morning. He loved that job because he loved being outside.

My mother passed away when I was just barely nine years old, leaving six kids at home. Mother died suddenly — we had no warning. She had a heart attack. Daddy was just torn up by her death. He really didn't know what to do because he depended on her for so many years that he sort of had to start a whole new life without her. With six kids at home, it wasn't a real easy job, I don't imagine. So the two older girls started taking care of old people in

53

the neighborhood — living in their homes from week to week and coming home on the weekends. That left just me to look after three of the boys at home. I was then ten years old but really it didn't seem like it was that hard at the time because when you are young, I guess you get used to a lot of things and you can accept things a lot easier.

One of my brothers was younger and two was older. We got along real good. We went to school and did what we were supposed to do and just sort of stayed there close at home. Daddy wasn't around much at that time because he was having some problems in relation to Mother's death. We sort of made it on our own with the help of neighbors and friends and all the sisters and brothers pulling together. We moved several times after Mother's death as Daddy took a tenant crop.

We six hung in there together. The older girls would come home on Friday nights and stay until Sunday. They would make sure we had clean clothes to go to school in. The older girl would give us a check to pay for our lunch and any school fees that we may have had. To be truthful, Dad wasn't there most of the time and some of the times we didn't know where he was — it was two to three weeks, sometimes a month, before we'd see him.

What cooking was done, I did. Mostly scrambled egg sandwiches in the evenings after school or cereal in the mornings before we went to school and we had our lunch at school. Of course, we got those state supported commodities, which came in handy. We kept a little bill at the nearby store where we got all of our groceries and at the end of the year we paid it.

There was a lady that lived down the road from us. She was really good about coming and showing us how to raise a garden, but the thing about it was, she wanted to take me away from my brothers. She didn't think it was normal for me to be there by myself with them boys. We were a very close family and we are still close today. There was no way I was going to leave them and they wouldn't leave me.

Then, I had a stepmother for fifteen years. I was fourteen when Dad remarried. I didn't like it much at first, because I guess I had gotten used to my ways of doing the housework. One day she sat me down and she said, "Let me tell you something — I don't intend to take your mommie's place. Or your place. As a matter of fact, I hate housework." She said, "You go ahead and do whatever you feel like doing — I'm here to please your daddy and that's all I intend to do." And that's exactly what she did for fifteen years. The other kids in the family, they thought she was lazy. But it turned out that two months after she was married to Daddy, she became really ill. We found out she was a diabetic and had kidney problems. She had a lot of trouble with sickness and later on cancer in the throat, but she was a very wonderful lady to my dad, which was all that mattered. Dad survived her too.

You know, she had no warning whatsoever that he had eleven children. He took her to Tennessee to marry her and she was twenty-three years younger than he was. She walks up the front yard and sees us kids standing in the door — well I can now imagine what she felt like then. She knew he had a family, but eleven kids is a great big shock when you don't know it. She helped me through a lot of my teenage courtships and was there for me. I really loved her for that and I always will.

About a year after she married Daddy, I still had some reservations about her being there so I went to live with my older sister who lived right out of Berea a little ways. Her husband was in the hospital and she was pregnant and needed some help and I needed some time away from my stepmother. I lived with her for about a year, then went back home and continued in school until the eleventh grade when I met my husband-to-be. Then I quit school.

I met him at a little store that was the local hangout for teenagers where we always run a bill. He'd already quit school when I met him — he was sort of a hippy type that wore mismatched clothes. He wasn't a bit handsome at the time but I knew I wanted to marry him the night I met him. And I did, several months later.

He was helping his stepfather farm part-time. We decided to get married in November of 1971, then on February the twelfth we were married. I quit school in January of that year and I was doing well in school. I had maintained a "B" average but for the most part I hadn't been socially active. I wasn't knowledgeable about things — like that I could transfer from one county school to the next. I should've looked into that but I didn't — I didn't know how.

We lived with his parents from the time we were married until

April, about two months. The landlord that owned his parents' farm had a little house in the back — about a half mile away in a barnyard. He told us that he'd let us live there for a year since we were just starting out if we would take care of the place. Then if we continued to live there, he'd charge us twenty-five dollars a month because the house wasn't in very good shape. But, it was home — it had four walls and a roof that didn't leak, which most of the houses I'd lived in did. It didn't have no rugs on the floor, but they were clean and it was good and warm in the winter time. It only had three rooms, but it was still ours.

I raised a big garden. Two days before we got married, Doug got a job at National Casket Factory in Lancaster. We were supposed to be married on Friday but he had come to me on Thursday night and said that we couldn't because he had to start work. Well, he needed a job and we needed the money, so we got married on Saturday.

My brother and my niece were our witnesses. We drove my husband's stepfather's car — a little '61 Ford Falcon and it quit right in the middle of Main Street. The witnesses were out pushing us down the street, trying to help us get home. The only money we had on us at the time was sixty-four cents. We stopped at the corner service station and bought sixty-four cents worth of gas to get to Garrard County — and we were finally home. We took it from day one and kept on going. We've had some rough going, rough times, but there have been some good times too.

I became pregnant immediately after we got married. My husband's mother was also pregnant, like me. She was due five weeks before me and had some rough problems with her pregnancy. Of course, she was in her mid-forties. I sort of took care of her house and family — she had ten children but only three were at home. So I sort of helped out there as there wasn't a whole lot to do at my house — nobody there and Doug worked all the time.

Then in May of that same year, he was laid off. Well, really, they went on strike. He'd only been there not hardly three months so he couldn't draw any kind of unemployment benefits, so we went back on those state commodities again, which helped out enormously. My main worry was how was I going to pay for this baby, so I went to the Human Resources Department and talked to a lady up there. They told me they could give me a medical card to pay for my hospital stay if I could pay for the doctor and we managed to do that. On August the sixth, my husband was called back to work at the casket factory and our son was born about six weeks premature on August the eighth. Most of the babies in my family were ten pounds or over. I weighed ten pounds, eleven ounces myself, so to have a seven pound boy didn't seem natural. He didn't have any hair on him and his fingernails weren't developed, but other than that he was healthy. He had his father's blood, which I was really thankful for because I have a problem with my blood.

I done real good. My mother-in-law always wanted me to stay in the house, but I couldn't hardly stand that. She believed the old way — you know, don't wash your hair after you have a baby, don't go outside in the sun and get cold, so I was stuck in the house for about three weeks. I was about to go crazy. Then, when my son was eight months old we moved to town to be more closer to Doug's job and a little bit bigger apartment. The lady across the street needed some help with her mother. She worked in Danville and her mother was a diabetic and didn't have any legs so she asked me would I stay with her mother. I said, "I would." I went over there at eight thirty every morning after I sent my husband to work and I stayed to twelve noon then I came back and fixed his dinner then would go back at one to stay to four o'clock. I worked there for almost a year and the good part about the job was I could take the baby with me. Mrs. B. was like sixty-something years old, but she was very alert and she loved kids because she never had any grand-children — her daughter never married. She was a very loving type of woman.

After a year staying with her, I started work at a local commu- nity clothing bank. At first I was a volunteer, just sweeping the floors, helping the boss out. Later on, she paid me two dollars an hour to come in whenever I could to do some cleaning.

My son started in Head Start and I didn't have a job. I mostly stayed home and volunteered to help at the local Sunshine Center in Lancaster any time they needed help. Doug was still working at the casket company. While Joel was in first grade, we got the chance to buy our own trailer by paying payments so we moved to Paint Lick and Joel started second grade down at the Paint Lick School.

We bought the trailer ourselves but it's on my grandfather's farm. We had an agreement that if I helped around his house, we could have our lot for the trailer rent free. We got it paid off within four years, but about a year before it was paid off, my husband's company closed down and he was off from work. He had worked there thirteen years.

Doug drew unemployment for a little over a year, then he got a job at Igniter Products in Danville and worked there about nine months, then that place closed down and went to Maine. So he's had some backsets — everybody closing down. It makes you sort of not want to do anything any more. When my husband kept being laid off, it seems like everywhere he went to look for a job the door was either shut in his face or they said, "You don't have an education" or something like that. He had stopped school when he was sixteen because at that time it was all the kids' idea that you quit school when you got sixteen because you just don't like it.

When we moved to Paint Lick I took care of his grandmother. She was an invalid and I kept her house. I didn't get paid for it until she became totally bedridden; then I was paid fifty dollars a week to go every day and look after her. She was on peritoneal dialysis and it was very tedious work. I was constantly with her; at one time there for three months, I was with her day and night. She couldn't be left alone and nobody else seemed to want to do it. It seemed like my whole day was filled up with her.

Then I became pregnant and I had a miscarriage. No insurance, no way to pay the doctor. The bill come in and my husband looked at me and said "Somebody's going to have to get a job." I mean, on a farm the money doesn't come every day — it comes in at the end of the year, but I had been told repeatedly by his grandfather that I wasn't smart enough to work. You know the old tale among farmers is that the wife's place is in the home. Well, the bills just kept mounting and there was this big hospital bill of mine. I felt like it was my problem, so the next day I went and asked for a job and I got one at Uncle Tom's Grocery. It was a complete restaurant and grocery where we served from eighty-five to a hundred people every day in a little room with seven tables and people would still stand in line. It was very popular. We had four full-time workers and three part-time because there was a whole lot to do. The place stayed open fourteen hours a day. That makes it sort of rough, to handle the whole business — you never know how much it is until you go into it yourself.

To start with I was just part-time. I was there about two weeks when the boss said, "Katie, you seem like you could use some extra time down here." I said, "Yeah, I'm here, I'm available any time you need me." By this time, my husband's grandmother had got so sick that I could no longer care for her. I couldn't handle it and then the problems with my miscarriage, too. I have some regrets about that because I never could make my peace with her. I had to start work and I knew she understood that. But, his grandfather never did and he never will — but it was the only way I could see to make a living. Even at forty-something dollars a week, that was money coming in. That's all we had at the time. I lived off of food stamps until my boss, who had owned a little antique shop next door, he came down one morning about a month after I had started at the restaurant and grocery and said, "What do you think about six days a week? Five hours a day?" I said, "I'm ready for it, if you think I can do it." He said, "You can do it and I've got to have somebody. I'm not going to be there — I'm going to run the antique store full time." So I worked more hours and was more the clerk instead of a waitress because the other women worked that. I took care of the main part of the store and done most of the ordering. I put down what I thought we needed and then he looked it over — I was sort of his assistant.

This was in 1986. That went on for about a year, then the lady that was hired ahead of me was having some family problems and she had five kids at home so she wanted to resign from her job and I was asked to take her place. I didn't think I could do what she had been doing but it really wasn't a whole lot more than what I had already been doing. It was just a little bit more extra hours and the pay was fifty cents more on the hour. I got to tell the other workers what to do. So I worked from eleven a.m. to seven p.m. for about three years.

In November of '88, I decided to get my GED. When I had first started working at the restaurant I met Mrs. Dean Cornett in the kitchen. She's a voice you won't ever forget once you hear it. I had known her when I was twelve or fourteen years old when I lived with my sister. She had helped my sister out a whole lot. When I heard her voice that day, I thought, "This can't be her." I walked back to look and just couldn't believe it was her as we had lost touch over the years. She said, "Is that really you, Katie?" Even though she lived in Madison County, she always come across the bridge to do her community work and Uncle Tom's restaurant was sort of her office. She'd get at a back table and spread out all of her papers and ask for some tea. She'd sit there for the better part of an evening doing community projects. She'd make little notes about who to help and what to do for them and if they needed some coal. She'd just ask people, "Can you load this for me and take this to that one?" And she'd have to make little memos. She was the one who come up with the idea of the GED program up at school on Tuesday nights. She didn't like it because I had quit school.

Well, I went and signed up — I wanted to see if I could do it. I went every Tuesday night from seven o'clock after I got off work until whenever for about six months and I obtained my GED. My husband was doing the same thing at the same time and he went right along with me. He didn't go as much as I did but he got his GED at the same time I did — we graduated together. I wanted to prove — I don't know if it's to myself or my husband — that I could do it.

During this time, my son was going to school. He finished high school then got married. His wife quit school as she had problems. Well, my son never moved out — he just brought her in, and I sure wasn't going to turn her out after all she'd been through. She was sixteen and sort of like the daughter I always wanted and never had — I wanted to protect her in every way I could. Right now my son is unemployed, got laid off six weeks ago. He worked for a man in Richmond as a handyman, doing outside work. He has been up to Danville to apply at a factory so I am encouraged.

Well, about six weeks after I got my GED a Professor Harry Brown from Eastern Kentucky University who comes regularly to Uncle Tom's asked me if Dean Cornett could get ten people to hold an English class would I be one of them. I said, "Sure, I'll try it." I got three girls on my own to come into class, so we made the quota and they gave us the class and Mr. Brown taught it. At first the GED classes were held at Paint Lick School, then Dean got into the process of trying to buy this empty building. Well, she got it and she's done quite a bit of work on it. It still needs an extensive amount of work but it's good enough for us right now and it's coming along every day. I wish there was more community support. Anyway, that's where we had our GED classes and the English classes Mr. Brown taught.

Several of us got financial aid through Eastern Kentucky University to pay for taking the class. I made a B, so in January I signed up for English II and to get financial aid to take that class. I made an "A" in it. Mr. Brown taught that one, too, right here in Paint Lick. Mr. Brown told me how good I was doing. I made an "A" on my term paper, that great term paper that I worked so hard on. It was on James Joyce, and I've got it in a frame right now, with my "A" on it and all of Mr. Brown's corrections and markings and all. Mr. Brown made it possible for me to attend another English class three mornings a week on the campus at Eastern Kentucky University if I could find time to get up there. Well, I did it and it was a lot of fun. I mean, just to get up in the mornings and go by myself into a building that contains three hundred rooms.

I'm fortunate that everybody's helped me — really fortunate. During the time I was taking the classes in English I and II, my boss was very supportive. He knew the college class started an hour before I got off work, so he said, "Go ahead, Katie, I'll take over for you." And he did and there was a lot of times he was really tired at the end of the day, but he would stay for me.

About this time I heard about the New Opportunity School — Dean Cornett mentioned something to me about it. It really didn't faze me because at that time I was doing my term papers and I was really enveloped in that. Through Dean's encouragement, I applied. I guess she saw my home life as something where I maybe was stuck. I really didn't know what it was like, to tell the truth, until I got out some. The more I worked in the college classes there at Paint Lick, the better I felt. Then when this New Opportunity School came into focus, I talked it over with my husband and I suppose he saw it as a threat. So the first session after I heard about it, I didn't even apply — there was just too much family problems. I mean I couldn't even bring up the subject without starting an argument with him. He saw it as a threat; I see that now.

When application time came around again for the winter session, I asked for one and got it just in time. I think I waited until the very last minute to send it in. I really wanted to get away from home because I thought it would do my family good and me, too. And it did — it helped them to know they'd have to do a little something on their own. Well, I had let the first chance to go to the New Opportunity School go by so when the second chance come I said, "Now this is it." I hid the application from my husband and I hid the fact that I talked to two different people for references.

Daddy always told us, "If you tell somebody you'll do something, you try your very best to do it. And you try to follow it through." I do try to do that but sometimes it gets so hard. But I try to keep my word. Well, I waited until I got accepted before I told my husband about it. The day I learned I'd been accepted, that was the first he found out because I just didn't have the courage to tell him.

When I got the phone call that I'd been chosen for the New Opportunity School, I just sat down on the floor — I was just exhilarated that somebody had enough trust in me to take me on.

The main thing I think I learned at the New Opportunity School was that my problems are not so big that I can't tackle them. And when you stop and look at the other ladies in the group with you, sometimes their problems are just as bad and maybe more so. It puts it in a perspective. You become friends with some wonderful women, and you are treated like an individual. That is of great importance, because it gives you some self-esteem — you are made to feel like what you are thinking, let alone doing, is going to be okay.

I went back home a changed person — more aggressive. I can laugh about things now instead of hanging my head. Like last night I told my husband I was coming up to Berea to talk to the people at the New Opportunity School this morning. He said, "What do you want to do that for?" I said, "Because I want to do it and I'm going to." Before the New Opportunity School, I would've hung my head and not even have mentioned it.

I've grown to be an individual and to me that is really important. After the New Opportunity School, I went back home and enrolled in another extension class in Sociology and still worked at

62

Uncle Tom's. Then about two weeks after I came back home, a job came open at our Post Office. My boss at Uncle Tom's was encouraging me to apply, and I remember saying, "John, I can't do that." He said "Yes, you can." He calls me Lady Katie — always has. There's not a day that went by since I started school that he's not said, "How are you today, Lady Katie?" He is a really special person.

While at the New Opportunity School I had learned to write a cover letter and resume and do research into certain jobs so when this Post Office job come up I didn't have much time to think. I had about twelve days to get everything ready before it was formally announced. I asked for an application and I got it and I had to have two references. I asked two elderly gentlemen where I worked at Uncle Tom's and they gave me real good references. My cover letter and resume were written and I walked into the U.S. Post Office and I said, "I want this job." And I got it. Through the New Opportunity School I learned to be direct and ask for what I want — I just knew I was going to get it before even I got there. You know, you have this little feeling that you know you can do it and it sort of transmitted right across the window at that Post Office.

Since then, my confidence has been built up time and time again. For a year now I have been Assistant Manager at Uncle Tom's, which is full-time and I work approximately fourteen hours at the Post Office. And I am still taking classes and got an A in Sociology.

Now my husband wasn't particularly supportive of my coming to the New Opportunity School, but he feels okay about that now. I think he really likes me, the new Katie. He may not love her, the new Katie, but he likes me. That's a start. He knows that I'm going to do whatever it is that I set my head to do, or I'm going to darn well try. I've been trying to re-evaluate my marriage and the problems in it. I can see it getting better. I don't want it to get worse. If you can recognize you have a problem, you can go to work on it and try to make it better.

When the Director of the New Opportunity School asked me to go to New York City with her to help raise money for the school, that was a big step. I asked Doug what did he think about it. "Do you think it would be all right? Do you think I'd do okay in New York City and me from the little old town of Paint Lick?" He said,

"Do you mind to re-phrase your question — instead just say — I'm going to New York City." Then he said, "Well, you'll make it." Well, when I got back, the only thing I remember him saying is, "You didn't call me when you got there." I didn't know how to call him, and I sure wasn't going to pay for it, because if it cost as much as the meals, I didn't need that. I think he is secretly proud of me; he just didn't want to say it. It would be admitting that he's not the main decision maker in the family.

I was surprised at myself — the fact that I rode on a plane, a jet. The fact that I mixed in with people I didn't even know that could have been murderers, you know, or anything. It was just real strange that I really went. I felt sort of let down when we got back on that jet to come back home. It's like I want to go home but yet I don't. I wanted to stay longer — I just didn't have enough time there. You know, at first I wasn't about to go to New York, but then I thought I wanted to help the New Opportunity School — maybe not with what I said but just my presence. And I wanted to help other women to get this same feeling of courage I had gotten.

Well, one thing after another started happening after I said I'd go. I was packing my clothes — I was going on a plane to New York City. I didn't tell a whole lot of people in Paint Lick — just a few close friends. I was having a lot of feedback, like, I'm not supposed to go. Women in a small farming community should stay home, you know. So I sort of slipped it by them. An elderly gentleman, when he found out I'd went and I'd come back said, "Katie, you didn't even give me time to worry about you." I said, "That's just one less worry you won't have, George." You see, in Paint Lick, you go because you NEED to do something, not because you WANT to.

I need and want to go to school. Within the next five years, I intend for life to get better. I don't want it to get any worse. It just takes determination and hard, honest work.

I would really like for Doug to be a little bit more supportive of himself. I'd say seventy-five percent of rural men do not have the "get up and go" to advance, to even want to. A woman, after being married ten to fifteen years, gets sort of bored with her life. I mean, she's had a baby, she wants to do something different because there's nothing to do but just the same old day-in and day-out stuff. I know a man gets tired of that, too — he's bound to. But, when a woman gets tired of it, she does something about it. A man just stays in there. That's the way it is in my family anyway.

Then, too, he considers women's liberation, women's rights, a little threatening. He sees women maybe taking over the world completely. I don't think that is going to happen but women need to have a big part in the world, I'll say that. If we were respected for our views, our opinions, for our brains, for our thinking — I think that would be all we'd need. You know, it's simple when you think about it.

(Katie is still working part-time at the post office and going to Eastern Kentucky University part-time. She has a GPA of 3.6 and has earned thirty-nine credit hours. Katie has recently taken a merit system test for a community outreach worker and hopes to get a job with the local health department.)

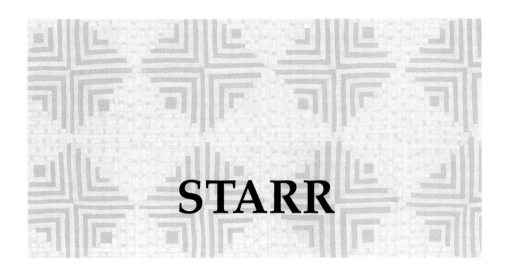

STARR

I was born in Letcher County close to Whitesburg. There was a whole bunch of us because my mom had been married and had three kids before she married my dad. We lived up at the head of the holler and had to walk out to school or ride the horse and sled out. My daddy was a coal miner. We had to get our own coal out of the coal mines behind the house.

It was really bad country. We would move every month. We moved to places like Sargent, Fleming Neon, Neon Junction, Thornton — every month we moved different places. When we moved to Owen County, that's when my mom got sick.

She had three strokes during surgery — they had given her up to die and called all the family in. She couldn't get out of bed; she was completely paralyzed on her left side. I'd have to go in and change her when she used the bathroom, and wash the sheets, and I was, like, maybe sixty pounds and was twelve years old. At the time I had one brother older than me and two sisters and a brother younger.

I had all the responsibility. I remember one time at one house we lived in, my half-sister and her husband lived upstairs over us. They were gone this one weekend, and I didn't have any food to cook for my sisters and brothers and my mom. She had to have something to eat, I knew that. I went upstairs, crawled up on this little roof-like thing, and took one of those little panes of glass out.

To show you how little I was, I crawled through one of those holes and got a pound of hamburger out of her freezer, crawled back out and put the window back in the best I could. And, you know, she never did mention it and I never did tell her. And that still bothers me. She died in 1983 and I never did tell her I stole that hamburger from her.

Mom could feed herself, but she couldn't get up and walk, and couldn't go to the bathroom by herself or anything. She would lean on me and kind of hop over in a chair while I changed the bed then hop back. She was a big woman — weighed one hundred and sixty to one hundred and seventy pounds easily. And my back would hurt so bad, I would just lay across the bed. When we'd get over to the bed, she would more or less fall on me, too. We'd fall on the bed and I'd think, "Oh, my back is going to kill me."

The worst part of it all was my daddy and his friends would come in and sometimes they'd bring their friends. You know how men are when they're drinking — grabbing and pawing at you and everything. I would take my younger sister and we would hide. We spent lots of nights in the closet and would fall asleep in there. You know, not very long ago my sister asked me, she said, "Was brother bothering you?" I used to say "Stay up with me," and she never knew why. But they was trying to get at her, too. I didn't know it at the time, but I was protecting her. I would hear them in the middle of the night: "Come over here and sleep with me. I'll buy you a bicycle." — saying things like that to her and she was only ten years old. They didn't say very much to me.

After my mom was paralyzed, she became pregnant and had another little boy. I only saw him one time and haven't seen him since. I don't know where he is or anything. I just know that the family that adopted him moved to Alabama.

When Mom went to the hospital to have the baby they didn't let her come back home and then the state came in and got us kids and took us away. During the time she was in the hospital one of the social workers came to school and got me and asked me to go out for a drive. I didn't know what was going on. She just said she wanted to talk to me about my family. She asked me all kinds of questions about what did we have to eat and I lied to her. I would tell her all this good stuff we had to eat and we really didn't have it.

I didn't know what to do. I thought Daddy'd get mad at me.

Well, they came to the house the day before the court hearing and said they'd be back the next day. And Daddy was trying to tell us, "Maybe they will put you in a better place. You'd be better off." The next morning they were back and this policeman came in with the social worker. He was standing there with the big gun and I was thinking, oh gosh, what's he going to do? kill us? or what? Ann and Bobby, they took off running. They were jumping fences and everything, trying to get away — running across these big fields. The policeman looked at my older brother and said, "Go get them." And, my brother said, "If you want them, you get them yourself." Them was his very words. That policeman chased them down and drug them back to the house.

Bobby was only five and Ann, she was ten. I was about twelve. And the hardest part was when we went in front of the courts. I didn't know what was going on. The day they took us to the courthouse there was a little baby sitting in a little infant seat. And I thought, oh my gosh, this is the prettiest little baby I've ever seen. I didn't know it, but that was my baby brother. Nobody had told us anything about him.

Well, they told us they's going to put us in another home because they didn't feel like staying with Daddy was right. Truthfully, it hurt because we was all going to be separated. But, I was thankful, I really was. That was the best thing that every happened to me in my life.

Well, John, he was sixteen, he was told he could stay with Dad. But Bobby was going with this one family — and it was so pitiful because I had changed his diapers and went to pre-school with him and he was more or less my kid. I had always taken care of him. And I was standing there on the street and he was hanging on to my leg and I was saying, "Now Bobby, you go with these people. They're nice people. They'll love you and take care of you and they'll buy you cap pistols," and, you know — that done it. He let go of me. But he kept looking back and he was crying.

Then, me and Ann, the sister closer to my age, went with these people to some place — to somebody's house — and they went and bought us an outfit of clothes and made us take a bath and put those clothes on. Then we went out and got in the car and they said we was going to Olive Hill, Kentucky. We got so sick. I guess because we was so nervous and upset and everything. We cried awhile and puked awhile — back and forth. And I kept imagining this big, old, red-headed woman with freckles all over and that she was going to be real mean to us. All kinds of thoughts went through our minds.

But we got there and went in and this lady was real tall and red-headed. But she wasn't fat, she was skinny. She had cooked, looked like, for a week. She had a big deep freeze in the kitchen and the table was set. She had country ham and mashed potatoes and everything. Pies — three or four different pies. And cakes — she had a feast ready for us. At that time, we were her first foster children. After that she had seven or eight more.

It was a big farm house and we had to work hard on the farm. We'd plant corn until two o'clock in the morning. We'd put in hay up until dark. Since I already knew how to cook, I had to spend most of my time cooking. I peeled so many potatoes that when I got married I had big callouses on my fingers. I'd say, well, why don't you let one of the other girls — she had two daughters and a son of her own — and I'd say, "Let one of them girls wash the dishes, it's their turn." And she'd say, "Oh, you do a much better job. You clean off the refrigerator and the stove — they don't do stuff like that. They don't do it to suit me, but you do." I always would have to make the biscuits and everything.

It was probably three or four months before I got to see any of my family. We more or less met in mutual towns. At first my dad wasn't supposed to know where we was or anything. Then later on, after they saw that it was going to be ok, that he wouldn't try to bother us or anything, we could write him letters.

Mother was in Lexington. At first they put her in the place where they put the crazy people down there — Eastern State Hospital. We went down to see her from the foster home and we walked in this place and they kept slamming these big doors and kept locking them behind us. There's some really strange people down there. People hollering and just falling out in the floor and screaming. I thought, oh, get me out of here. I don't want to be here. That was the worst experience of my life. You know, Mother wasn't crazy at all. I don't know why they put her there. She finally ended up in a

70

nursing home in Ohio. I never seen her any more until I got married. I saw Daddy one time while we was in the foster home.

My dad died last year. When Daddy died he was in the same nursing home. He came up in 1981 or '82 to visit Mom and he checked himself in. He had had two or three heart attacks himself and I think he had high blood pressure. He died of a massive heart attack. They called me like at two o'clock in the morning. My sisters were there but they didn't tell Mom. We took her into a little room and I asked them, "Well, do you all want to tell her?" And they kept looking at me like, Go ahead. So, I said, "Mom, Dad's gone." And she didn't understand me at first. She acted like, Yeah, he's not here. And I said, "Mommie, Daddy died." And she just looked at me and it seems like all the blood just drained out of her face. She looked at me for the longest time. And she grabbed me and started crying and it was a really bad time. She started vomiting. Still yet she'll say, "Daddy's gone, Daddy's gone." You can understand her say that. She was only thirty-nine when she had the stroke and now she's sixty-two.

I was having to fork out everything for Daddy's funeral. My brother was in jail at this time. I had made thirteen or fourteen phone calls before I finally located where he was. I had to pay ninety-four dollars to get him to be able to come. And he could just come when the funeral started and as soon as the funeral was over, he had to leave. He had to wear shackles. The guard that brought him and stayed with him, I had to pay for his time. Nobody wanted to pitch in and help me pay for nothing. I had to have a money order waiting for the guard or he was going to take him back. You know, my brother never did call me and thank me. I haven't seen him since. At the funeral I told him, I said, "Call me sometime and write to me." He was my youngest brother and was only five when they came to take us to the foster homes. You know, there were times when Dad would say, "I started to just come up and just steal you kids, bring you back home." And then he'd say, "Well, you was probably better off with the others." I think he knew it wasn't really a fitten place with him. He wasn't able. He had a wooden leg. When he was twenty-one, his dad shot him in the leg and he had to have his leg amputated way up on his thigh. So, he wasn't in all that good a shape anyway. He worked in the coal mine and all with

71

that wooden leg.

I don't think we ever became a family. We was all together at my daddy's funeral. Me and Betty, we're still pretty close. We write to each other and keep in touch. But my sister in Florida, I haven't seen her since 1980. When I got out of the car at Daddy's funeral, she said, "Oh, I hate you, you're so skinny." That was the first thing she said to me after all those years. I had gotten a shirt from the Mini Mall for a couple of dollars and a white blouse I had had for five years that I got at the Dollar Store and a blazer from a used clothing store. And they would say stuff like, "Well, how much did that outfit cost you?" And this at my daddy's funeral.

So the foster home family really became my family. I still go up and visit them.

Well, I was silly, you know. I fell in love. I was dying to get married after we graduated from high school. My sister, they were paying for her to go to beautician school because that's what she wanted to do. They bought her a kit for fifty dollars and got her started but she wouldn't finish it. She dropped out of school. I was the only one that graduated from high school out of the whole bunch, even the foster family's own children.

As soon as I finished high school I got married. We had started dating when we were juniors and became engaged when we were seniors. We graduated on one Sunday, and the following Saturday, we got married. He had a job working night shift. He blew up a car hurrying home to see me. We were married almost ten years and had the two boys.

I was working where he was working; I made car parts. I worked there for awhile and then we moved to Georgia and he worked on construction. We didn't stay there very long because we moved back home to Olive Hill and I started working at a sewing factory. The part that I worked in made shirts and I worked there five years. When my second boy was born, in 1980, it was the hottest summer I ever remember. I was so big anyway, I quit. I asked for a layoff until the baby was born, and after he was born, I didn't go back. Then I just worked in grocery stores and here and there. Petty jobs.

After being married for ten years we were divorced. Then I jumped right into another marriage. We went together about seven

72

months before we got married — then Dawn was born. My husband was a truck driver. We were living in Olive Hill in 1984 and when his mother died she willed us a house near Richmond, a farm. We were trying to keep the upkeep of the farm going and the house in Olive Hill, too, and we would come down to Richmond on the weekends. I loved it down here — I really wanted to move down here. Finally, he got a transfer from Olive Hill to Lexington. He was staying at the farmhouse through the week, working in Lexington and then he would come home on the weekends. He had a little girl also, that he had custody of, so here I had four kids. It was hard being up there all week and finally he said, "Why don't we just move down to Berea?" We moved down here and everything started happening. I started working at K-Mart and at a real estate office selling houses. I was trying to take care of the family and work. The thing of it was, every time I would make sales calls — you have to make them after hours, after people got home from work and after they had dinner and everything. Well, I'd get ready to go and he would get furious and ask, "Where are you going?" He was just so jealous, like I was going out to meet somebody. And I'd say, "I have to go see these people, they made this appointment." He would always act like he didn't believe me at all. Then, he got so he'd be staying out until two in the morning.

He would read my speedometer — how many miles I had put on. Even when I was working at K-Mart he would call over there and ask the girl I worked with how many men came in there that day. One day, I had worked all day and my truck was parked right beside my friend Shelly's car. That night, it was real cold and her car wouldn't keep going. She'd pull up a little piece and it would just quit. And I didn't want to just leave her stranded, so I followed her down the road to her turnoff, to make sure she got home okay. Well, when I got home he said, "Where you been?" And I told him about the trouble Shelly was having with her car. He said, "Did you lock the truck?" And I said, "No, but I'll go back and do it." He said, "No, you sit down here and have a cup of coffee and I'll go out and do it." He come back in and slammed the door and said, "Where in the ____ have you been today?" I said, "You know where I've been." He said, "You have put sixty something miles on that truck." I said, "Honey, you read that wrong because I didn't." I told Shelly about it and she said, "Golly, what is his problem?" He was always so jealous. And come to find out, he had been seeing this other woman for a long time. I didn't find out about it until I left him. Then everybody started saying, did you know that he's been seeing her for three or four months?

I moved out. It was the hardest thing I've ever done in my life. I thought it would be better on me, him, and the kids. I said, "We're not happy and me being accused over and over is not right." So, I took all the kids and left. Even his daughter cried and wanted to leave with me. He said to her, "You might as well go. I'd have to pay a babysitter anyway, so you might as well go with her." So I took all four kids and rented this two bedroom apartment. I slept on the couch, the boys slept in one room and the girls slept in the other room. We lived there twenty-eight days. I was having to pay two hundred and fifty-five dollars a month, plus two hundred and fifty dollars deposit. I had to come up with all this money. But, a lot of people were helping me and I was working at a laundromat.

My job at the laundromat was attendant. I had to wash people's laundry when they brought it in, and sell supplies. At first I was working at McDonald's and at the laundromat. I'd go into McDonald's like at six in the morning, work until three thirty p.m. and the owner of the laundromat, she would come and pick me up at three thirty and I would run in the bathroom and wash up the best I could and change clothes and be at the laundromat at four o'clock to start working. I didn't have a car during that time. I'd finish then at nine thirty or ten, sometimes it was after ten and she would bring me home at night. The kids had to get on the school bus by themselves. The owner of the laundromat, she'd keep Dawn while I was working at McDonald's and then I'd go to the laundromat and just keep Dawn there at the laundromat with me until closing time. There would be times when I would go home and the electric would be turned off. The kids would be sitting there in the dark with flashlights. My husband was supposed to be paying it and when I'd ask him about it he'd say, "Yeah, I paid it. I don't know why they turned it off." There was times when we didn't have anything in the refrigerator. I went out lots of times and picked poke greens and had cornbread and ice water and fried potatoes. A friend would come out and bring coffee and rolls, doughnuts, sugar, milk — things like that. He knew we needed it.

I made sure we had food before anything else. My husband asked me once, "Well, how are you doing on your own?" And I said, "You know, we haven't been without milk since we left you."

I had to quit working at McDonald's — it was too much for me to work at both places. But, I stayed on at the laundromat and worked more hours there after that. I worked from eight in the morning until ten at night.

That first apartment we moved in, it was so expensive. That's when I had all four kids. But he only let his daughter stay a week with me. But, anyway, me and my three kids stayed at that apartment about twenty-eight days and then Ms. W., the director of the Housing Authority, she called me and said, "I've got an apartment for you if you want it." She told me how much it was and I thought, "Yes, definitely, I'll take it." So we moved over there and it was a really nice place. It had four bedrooms, a bath and a half, a huge kitchen and living room. I thought, gosh, I've never seen so much room.

Then I went to work at a factory but I only worked there like three weeks and I got real sick, almost passed out. The lady that runs the laundromat, she came and got me and took me to the doctor. He just sent me on to Pattie A. Clay Hospital to the emergency room up there. They did ultrasounds and stuff and found out that my gallbladder was really inflamed. He said it was like I had a bag of rocks in there. They sent me home for a week to take antibiotics before I could have surgery done. I had forty-one gallstones.

I came home and I was sitting around trying to recuperate and here come my friend Rhonda and she said, "I've got the thing for you."

I said, "What?"

And she goes, "Oh, I was talking to the woman who directs the New Opportunity School for Women and I think you really should do this."

I said, "What's it for?"

"It's for women in your situation," she said.

And I said, "Well, what do I do?"

She said, "You'll have to fill out this application. You have to write this essay about why you want to go."

I said, "But I don't really want to." And she said, "Well, at least just fill it out. Just think about it." I was recovering from surgery and just too tired to sit up very long or anything. I would walk from the living room to the bathroom and I would just be so tired I couldn't move.

So I just pushed the papers over to the other side of the couch and then in a day or so here she came back over. "Have you got that filled out yet? I'll take it to Mrs. Stephenson." And, I thought, "Here she comes again, she's going to talk about the New Opportunity School."

But, just to please her, I thought, well, I probably won't get accepted anyway, but I'll please her and fill it out. I can't even remember what I wrote. My sister came down and she stayed a couple of days with me. I said, "Read this and see how it sounds to you. Does it sound okay?" And she said, "Yeah, it sounds good." And as I said, I don't even remember what I wrote but then my friend brought me down to Berea College to talk to Mrs. Stephenson. Then I started getting excited about it. I couldn't believe it when I was told I had been accepted. I was scared to death. Oh here I was, I got accepted, and now that I am, gosh, I'll probably go down there and make a fool of myself. I don't know how to do anything and what about if they ask me to do something and — well, I was just really hyper.

Then I thought, what will I do with my kids now? So I talked to their daddies and got everything squared away — who was going to keep them.

Once I got there, I felt real comfortable. But I really didn't have any confidence. I was just a good faker. Being around the other women, seeing that I wasn't the only one in my situation, that other people had been through it too, helped me. Anita Barker, our counselor, she really made an impression on me. She said, "It's out there, just go get it." And she just kept pounding that into our heads. I don't know — it must have made me realize that there is something else out there. I don't have to sit back and wait for somebody to bring it to me because that won't happen. You have to go out and dig and go for it yourself.

During the school we all had jobs and mine was at the hospital. When I said I wanted to do something at the hospital no one had ever been placed there before. So, I said, well, maybe I'd like to have something to do with teaching. So, that's what I was expecting and when I got to the school and got my folder and it said "Hospital Lab" I thought, All right!

I stayed there about two weeks and my third week there I ran into the director of Respiratory Therapy. I had known her because she used to come to the laundromat where I worked. And I said, "Well, hi," and she said, "What are you doing here?" And I told her I was just hanging out in the lab and she goes, "Well, why don't you get into something where you can make some money?" I said, "I'm open for suggestions." And she said, "Why not Respiratory Therapy?" And I said, "Sounds good. Can I come up and watch you all? See what you do?" And she said, "Sure. Come on up in the morning."

I watched them, and walked around the hospital with them and the director said, "If you're really interested in this, there's a school in Rockcastle County and the instructor is going to be here in the morning. I'll introduce you and maybe you can get into the school there." And I said, "Okay." So, sure enough, he came in and he was really super nice. He asked me to write my name and address and phone number down and he said he'd get information to me. And I thought, sure that sucker will — he'll put my address in that big briefcase and never find it again. You know, that's how those things work. It was only like three days or four and I got this big package in the mail from the vocational school. I tore into it and started filling out all these applications. I had to have my birth certificate and shot records, letters of recommendation and pictures of myself. I had to get all of that taken care of and get it in. Then I had to take an adult educational test and pass that. There was some one hundred and forty or one hundred and fifty applicants trying to get in and they only chose twenty-five and I was one of them. I was so excited, but the program didn't begin until the following January so meanwhile I went back to work at the laundromat until I could get into school.

Well, I was going to school and not working and in February I started doing clinicals at the hospital, just a month after I had started school. In June the director of the department called me and said, "Are you ready to come to work for me?" And I said, "Yeah, I guess I am. When do you want me?" And she said, "In the morning."

So I was going to school forty hours and working twenty-four hours on the weekends and taking care of the kids and studying and making good grades. There was times when I felt like, I can't do this. I worried a lot. I had to really study hard. It was really hard for me to try to concentrate with the kids around. Mommie this, and Mommie that. Lots of times I would read on the tape recorder, play it back. I would study after the kids went to bed. I would put them to bed at nine and I would study until eleven or twelve and then I would get up at five in the morning and study until time for me to leave. It took about forty minutes to drive down there. I'd go to school all day and get home about four thirty and cook, wash dishes, help the kids with their homework, make sure everybody had their baths, their clothes laid out, because in the mornings I would have to leave like at five a.m., sometimes five thirty, according to where I was doing clinicals — sometimes in Corbin, or Lexington. Lots of times we'd carpool. The kids would get themselves up and they only missed the bus one day the whole thirteen months I went to school.

My kids have really been good about cooperating and helping. I wouldn't have been able to make it without them, I don't think. My fourteen year old, he complained a lot. "All I ever do is babysit. Never get paid." The other two had to be cooperative with him to make it work. There was times that if I didn't have to go to school one day, or I was off from work for some reason, they would bring me breakfast in bed. They are very special kids.

In November, we had to take the Kentucky Vocational Educational Test. We had to pass this in order to graduate. Right before we got out for Christmas break, we took it. We had to wait two weeks for the results. When I did get it, my son brought it in. I said, "Oh my God, I can't open that," and he said, "What is it?" and I said, "That's my test results." And I was down in the floor in the hallway sorting laundry and he said, "Well, go ahead and open it, Mom. Let's see." I started crying. I was praying, Oh God, please let me pass this. I've gone this far, don't let me down. And finally I said, "Well, I might as well just look." Before I could get up the nerve to look, he screamed in my ear, "Mom, you passed, you done it." He grabbed it. He just squeezed me to death. And he said, "Here, let me see what you made." I said, "I don't care what I made, just that I passed." But I did make a ninety-eight on it.

Then we had to go to Louisville for the National Boards for Respiratory Care. I couldn't force myself to pick up a book to study. I had all the notes, all my notebooks laid out and everything. But I could not study at all. I was so burned out. Like I was just brain dead, you know. I didn't want anything to do with any more books. I had tapes and it seemed like every time I would turn on those tapes the kids would come in the house and start making noise and I said, I might as well shut it off.

When we went down to Louisville to take it, there was about four or five of us girls that went together. It took three hours to take the test. I got up and my legs were stiff and I was light headed. It was a rough time, but we had to wait six weeks to get these results. Talk about ulcer time. I had them for real. When this test come back, I went out and got it and I laid it on my desk and I said, "I'm not going to open it. I'll let somebody else open it." Well, my son came in. He said, "I'll open it," and grabbed it and I said, "I'll open it myself." Because I was afraid if I had failed that he'd say, "Yeah, Mom, you failed it. I thought you was doing so good." And if I failed it, I wanted to be the first one to see it. I tore into it and I started bawling again. I had passed it. A friend of mine called me and said, "What's wrong?" And I said, "I've just gotten my test back from the National Board." She said, "You did? How'd you do? Did you fail it?" "No, I passed it," I told her and she said, "Well, what'd you make on it?" I said, "Ninety-two." Even the youngest child, she patted me on the back and said, "Way to go, Mom."

So I started working part-time last June at the hospital while still in school, then after I finished they started giving me more days. Then they offered me full-time work with benefits and the whole works, dental and everything. After I became certified, I got a raise. My pay was pretty good in the beginning but then I started working nights and that was a dollar an hour more. Then I got a good raise and I was going to have to move from the apartment because it was for low income and now I had raised my income and was making money. Ms. W. came and told me I was going to have to pay three hundred and eighty dollars a month when I had been paying like fifty dollars a month. That's a big chunk. She said, "You don't seem surprised." I said, "No. You know Uncle Sam."

Around that time, that's when I met Bill at the hospital. We started talking and going out and one thing led to another and he proposed — I think he proposed. He just told me, "Well, this is the way it's going to be — you're going to marry me." He was a computer specialist at night at the hospital. We got married in July. Before we got married he brought this book of house plans — blueprints — up to the department. And he said, "Look through these and find out which house you'd like to build." Come to find out, I picked out the house that he'd picked out, so he sent off to get house plans for that one. Then we were riding out in the country to see where we wanted to build this house. That's when I saw his great-grandfather's house and we decided to move there and fix it up and try to live there until we found the right spot where we wanted to build. That way we wouldn't have to hurry into something and make a decision too fast. I'd like to live out in the country and he would, too. The kids love it out there. We've got my three kids and his two sons living with us, along with three cats and looking for a dog. I want a big collie dog — Lassie.

I've really been blessed. My husband's very considerate. He always wants to do what's right for me first before anything else. He's the type of person when you come in and are so tired and cranky and don't want to be bothered, he says, "Would you like for me to rub your feet?"

Mother is still in the nursing home in Olive Hill. I see her a couple of times a year. She is a real bad diabetic and still paralyzed. She can't see out of her left eye and can't hear out of her left ear. You know, her whole left side is just dead. You can't understand a lot she has to say and when you give her paper to write, it kind of drifts away and just runs together. You can't read what she writes. There's one thing for sure — I'll go in and I'll sit down on her lap and say, "Hi Mom. Am I your favorite daughter in the world?" And she'll just grab me and start kissing my whole face. And she'll say, "Love you, love you, love you, love you." That I can understand! She is so special.

It seems like I always had to be able to take care of myself.

Everybody says, "You're so bubbly and bouncing around," and "You've been here working all night long and you come in and you're just smiling." Lots of times I smile when I really don't feel like it. But I don't want pity. I think that takes a lot away from a person. There's lots of times when I don't talk about myself. Somebody will go, "How are you?" and I'll say "Everything is just fine." But really, deep down, God, I'm hurting. But when you get out talking to people, you find out that somebody is in worse shape than you are. And you think, here I am pitying myself when there's worse things out there.

I guess that's the reason I smile — because I want everybody else to be happy, too.

(Starr is currently living out West working in respiratory therapy in a large city hospital. She owns her own home. Her oldest son is starting his third year in college and her other two sons are doing well in school, winning awards for good grades.)

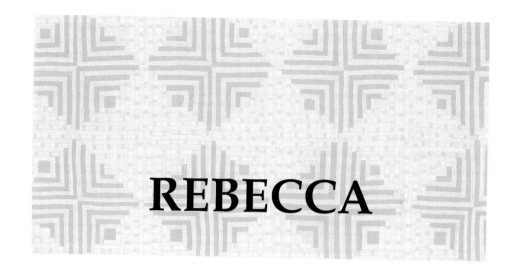

REBECCA

I was born in Paint Lick — my father helped deliver me. I have two brothers and a sister, all older than me, but I really wasn't very close to them because I was a lot younger. I had no problems except just trying to get along with my brothers and sister, because they tried to boss me around a lot. My sister would try to make me wash the dishes and we would fight every time Mama would leave. My brother would throw all my things in the pond when he would get mad at me. That's more or less how they punished me because Mama and Daddy never punished me at all. Because I was the baby of the family they all kind of resented me just a little bit — and they still do. They say that I got by with a lot more than they did because Daddy was a lot stricter with them. But all in all, we got along okay.

I had a happy childhood. One of my first memories is of my mama taking me to a special program for women and their children at a church in Berea. Women could come to the church and bring their children every Friday and stay all day. I was about four years old when I started going with Mama. I can remember coming down the steps and smelling the soup and food cooking and everybody laughing and talking. It was just a happy atmosphere. Everybody was willing to help each other and it served a purpose as far as people getting clothes they needed. If they needed clothes for their new babies, they made layettes and did things for the fami-

83

lies when there was no help. They always made quilts to help people who needed them and sometimes made quilts and clothes for their own families.

My mother and a lot of the people who came had to walk to get there. I guess some people walked twenty miles back and forth to get there even in cold weather. You worked on quilts, or in the nursery, or cooked during the mornings and you got four tickets for the time you were there then you could only get four clothing items for those tickets. You had to buy your lunch with one ticket. Then it was a mad scramble for people to get what they wanted. Everybody would pick out something that they saw early in the morning that they wanted and made sure that they got that. There were a few fights every now and then. But, you know, people were more desperate for clothing items and it was almost like Christmas every Friday. Mama would come home with stuff for the family and everybody would run to see what she had.

When I had my own family, I started going and I'm still going. If you don't go you feel like you're missing something. I brought my two youngest with me. They remember it and enjoyed it, so it's become a tradition. I worked in the nursery to help because my children were in there. I didn't like to sew that much but I did tack quilts every now and then after my kids got older. I don't work in the nursery anymore, but I enjoy tacking quilts because I get to visit and talk to everybody. Now they have plenty of clothes — there's no limit as to what you can get. You don't have to have tickets any more, they just say, "Go shopping." And you go shopping and take what you want — they have a lot of good donations. It's something to look forward to because you get to meet your friends and have a devotional. Sometimes there are get-togethers — potluck suppers and dinners and arts and crafts programs, too.

My mother and daddy, they moved around a lot. My dad liked to trade and buy places. I went to a lot of different schools as we lived a lot of different places, which I didn't mind. I enjoyed meeting new people and that was good for me because I made friends pretty easy.

My first school was a two-room school. My mother always cooked at the school so she could keep up with me — make sure I was being taken care of. I just lived eight houses up the road from the school. Something I remember that was a real pleasant memory of my school days was on a day near summer time. It had been raining and outside there was a pine tree. There was a mother deer and her little baby came out and was standing there and it was raining and sun shining together and our teacher let us get up and look out the window. That was a good memory. Also, when I was going there to school there was a woman named Henrietta Childs would come to our school. We loved to see her come because she told us stories and had all these little toy animals with her. She would read to us from books and show us the little animals.

I liked school and was doing well up until the tenth grade. I was riding the bus to the county high school then. I had started working at a local restaurant when I was fourteen and had a little paycheck. Then I got interested in boys and I just didn't like school after that. My girl friend and I were waitresses. I sometimes worked in the evenings after I got out of school. We'd get off the bus at the restaurant coming from high school. I made fifty cents an hour. I continued on into school up into the eleventh grade and continued working at the restaurant. But I started skipping school, my girlfriend and I, because when we'd get paid we'd want to go spend our paycheck. We started missing a lot of school and then I got pregnant during that year of school. My girlfriend and I were both pregnant at the same time. We were in the bathroom where we worked talking about it and someone overheard us. The lady that was over us took us upstairs and talked to us and told us we couldn't work any more. That was a pretty bad time because it was kind of unexpected for both of us. We were pretty shocked about losing our jobs. That was the first experience we had about facing life — the real world. Up until then, everything was just fine.

I didn't tell my mother that I was pregnant until I was almost five months. But she realized it. She was asking a lot of questions. But I didn't even realize that I was pregnant at first. Mama said I had to talk to them at school and had to get married. So I went to school and told them and I quit two weeks before school was out for the year. I guess my mom and dad was pretty disappointed in me. I didn't want to get married. I wanted to keep working and raise the baby by myself. But that was not done back then. So, I got married because they insisted. We lived with my mother and dad up until the baby was born. They have helped me a lot.

My husband was nineteen and I was seventeen. He had quit school in sixth grade. He worked on car bodies and things like that in a garage. Soon after the birth of the baby, I was pregnant with another child — and it was just the same thing right over and over because I didn't even think about my future at that time, my future was raising the children. I had always wanted babies but I didn't think about it happening that way because I just didn't know about life. Mama and Daddy never talked to me about anything. They just said, "Always be good and don't get in trouble." I didn't know what that meant. I thought I was being all right, and I didn't know what I was doing could get me in trouble.

I remember long about the last month of school while I was still going we had a home economics teacher trying to tell us about the facts of life. But I still didn't understand the way they was telling it to you. It was more or less just kind of beating around the bush. Biological. Maybe if I'd had more school I would have understood it more, but at the time, I didn't.

I went back to work at the restaurant after my son was born and worked for a little while until I had my second child. From 1964 up until 1971 I had four children. They was born about two years apart. During that time I helped my mother do housecleaning some because she had always done that kind of work. I knew that wasn't for me — that wasn't what I wanted to do, but I did it. From the time I was seven years old, I helped with the neighbors and everybody. I would go to their homes and help cut their hair and comb it and help them do their housework. When I was twelve years old, I stayed with a lady at night. I made a quarter every night.

When my children were little, I was totally content just being with them. If I had of had a good marriage, I would have never thought about doing anything else except raising my family and staying home until they all got grown. But then right before my fifth child was born, I just happened to be driving by the hospital and every time I would drive by there I felt like I needed to go in and see if there was some kind of training I could get into. From the time I was real small I knew I wanted to be a nurse. I heard people say when you got older you changed your name. I said, "I'm going to be a nurse and change my name to Mary." The day I did stop at the hospital they was starting the nurse aide training courses. The nurse that helped deliver my daughter was the woman that was giving the nurse aide classes. I already knew her and that kind of helped me to get in. This was a six-weeks course and they promised a job at the hospital when it was over. The course was free and we had to go every day. We had on-the-job training for just a week and after that we worked on the floors.

They hired me directly at the hospital after my training was over. I really liked it. If I had just known that I could have gotten more training by going on to more classes I would have stayed there, but I didn't really talk to anybody about it. So I went on to work at Madison Manor Nursing Home where I could learn how to give medicine and do other things there. I kind of regretted that I ever quit the hospital. I should have stayed there and they would have helped me go on to more courses but I didn't know that then. I learn as I go.

My husband, he was an alcoholic, so we just had our homes for a while and then we'd live with my mother for a while. We moved around a lot. We were never really stable. We didn't really have a home, and anytime we got in trouble, he'd go to his mother's and I'd go to my mother's with all the children and stay there. More or less, my mom and dad helped raise the family. That's just how it was because he was just never responsible for them. I was the one having to make the living and I did it because I knew I had to. My mom helped keep the kids while I worked. Then after a while, my older ones were getting old enough that they could help babysit. My oldest daughter, she was more or less the mother. My kids have said they thought she was their mother because they saw her more than they did me because I was working two jobs a lot of the time.

I worked in a nursing home in Lexington for almost a year. I would have to leave home at four in the morning and get home at four in the evening. I had gotten divorced and remarried and my husband wanted to move to Lexington, which we did for a while. I worked at a motel for a while. But I didn't stay in Lexington but about six months. None of my children would go up there with me to live except my daughter and she was young enough that she couldn't make the decision not to go. I could live anywhere, you know. I love to travel and love to meet people and I love different jobs. I love learning things. But my children depend on my mother and dad to take care of them if things get bad. They are now twenty-six, twenty-four, twenty-three, nineteen and fifteen. Just the fifteen year old is living with me now.

None of my children have finished school. They all quit. My oldest got married and moved to California when she was fifteen. My two boys are working on their GEDs and are really having a hard time getting it. They have been about a year trying. My oldest boy goes down to the GED Center when they have classes there, but he just goes and takes his tests to see what he can do on it. My other son, he has just been going and taking the tests without studying either. They are finding out if you don't study and have a teacher, you can't hardly pass it, but they are getting closer to passing.

Just after my last child was born I went to the vocational school to get my GED. I found out when I started applying for jobs that they wanted to know if you finished high school and I hadn't. I felt that I needed it. Then my daughter that had just came back from living in California went to get her GED and she passed and only had a ninth grade education. So I felt like if she could get it, I knew I could. She kind of inspired me because I felt bad not having mine and she had gone to get hers.

I passed my GED the first time. I'll admit I guessed on some of the answers but I suppose I guessed right. I hadn't thought much about going back to school or anything until my daughter got older. I was still working full-time and just more or less making a living, but I didn't know where to start to go to school. I had often wondered, where do I start looking for a way to further my education? I had thought of vocational school because I worked for a lady that was one of the counselors at the vocational school, and she was giving me some information to try to get in. Then I would get caught up in daily living and things that were going on with my kids going through their teen years and I didn't really have time to think about myself.

Then I read about the New Opportunity School in the newspaper. I thought about trying to get in but I was afraid to do so on my own. I figured, "Well, just forget that. Maybe I'll try it next year if it comes back again." But the women at church wouldn't hear of that. They insisted that I get an application and fill it out — they encouraged me to do it. When I was accepted, I was real pleased that I went through with it. You are so afraid that you won't be accepted because you think that you're not good enough, you know.

Then I got scared when I got accepted. I thought, "Well, I don't even know where to start." I thought, "What opportunities would there be for me anyway, because I've already been out there and I've lived a lot and done a lot of things." You know, how do you start again when you've messed your life up so bad?

The most helpful thing that happened at the New Opportunity School was getting my confidence back. That was the biggest thing. And I was able to meet new friends and find out that other people were in the same position I'm in and they had gone through a lot of similar things, although different situations. But, we all felt the same about ourselves. We felt like we had no purpose and had messed our lives up really bad and there was no hope for us, although, down deep inside there is a survival instinct. We're always looking for something, whether we know it or not.

So we found out while at the school that we were capable of doing a lot more than we thought. It gave me insight to a lot of things that I hadn't thought about for a long time in my personal life. The counseling helped a lot. It gave me the confidence I needed to start back out in the world again and pick up kind of where I'd left off after raising a family and learning a lot about life. With my family I've had to go through a lot at a young age when I shouldn't have. But it was meant for a purpose — you don't do those things unless it's meant to be, I guess. We find out we're stronger than what we ever thought we was.

I still know that I want to be in the nursing profession. That's my life's work. I don't know where it's going to lead, but I'm looking forward to a lot of things but I don't know for sure where I'm going to end up. I talked to a lady about how to get in a nursing program but that was last year and so many things started happening and I didn't get back. I'm planning on trying to get my ACT test done within the next few weeks if I can. But I don't think I could carry a full course load since I need to work part-time and go to school part-time. I've got to find out about if I can do that.

Right now, I'm working at night and then I also work during

the day three days a week for my daughter, babysitting. That's not what I want to keep doing because I'm away from home fifteen hours a day. I go down to her house at seven thirty in the morning and get off at four thirty in the evening. Then at six I go to work at my other private nursing job until ten at night. I'm not going to do that much longer. I've got to make some changes pretty soon.

My fifteen year old is in middle school now and in classes they have for people that are having problems learning. That kind of helps her because they let them work at their own pace and they can keep up with each other and can do better if they are not having to compete with the people who are doing a lot better than they are. They are real good at the school to work with Joyce. They've been real lenient with her because she has been having a lot of health problems. They are trying to help her all they can and now she goes to see the counselor at school and talks with her. Since she has missed a lot of school, she also now has a court-appointed worker that helps her. She is something like a social worker and helps her stay in school. If she has problems, she calls her and talks to the social worker. It's just the simple fact that my daughter doesn't feel good. She just can't get up in the mornings and do things because she is having a heart problem that was diagnosed just two months ago as mitral valve prolapse. But she has had it since she was ten and it leads to panic attacks. They don't know why she is having them. The doctor has kind of told her it was all in her head, but I don't agree with that at all, and I'm going to get a second opinion. She's had the heart monitor done and an EKG and it showed up negative. I'm glad that nothing showed up, but there is still something there that they have not found.

My other children have talked with my daughter and tried to encourage her to stay in school because they all say, "Look at us, we can't get a good job because of no education and we're having problems." But she really has no choice. She has to go until she is eighteen or finishes high school. They don't give them a choice now. Even though she may not want to go, she is going to have to.

I have to see my family through some of these hard times but there is going to be a time for me. I hope soon. Just in the last year seems like everything has happened and I've not been able to get on with what I've wanted to do. A few years ago I wouldn't have even kept thinking of going on and furthering my education and doing things for me. I was so wrapped up in my family's problems, but now they are getting older and out on their own.

Both my sons lucked out and got good jobs. They are both working in grocery stores. One is an assistant manager of the meat department but he could be manager if he wanted to be but he chose not to be. My other daughter is at home with her new baby. She has a learning disability. That is a problem, but she has a good husband and he helps her a lot because she's twenty-three years old but is seven years behind in her mind. She is a good mother and a good home-maker and is happy doing that and her husband is happy with her doing that. They live in a trailer park and have the one child that is just two months old. She quit school in the ninth grade — she dropped out of school and just kind of got lost in the shuffle. They didn't keep track of her, and I didn't report that she had quit. You can't get by with that now. If only she had stayed in school they could have helped her with her learning disability but she lost out by quitting. She is happy being a wife and mother. She depends on me still for a lot of things, but she is growing up now that the baby has been born — she has changed a lot.

I'll still be here for my family for quite a few more years. I'm not happy with my work hours or my money because I'm just barely making it, you know, for all the hours I'm working. I don't choose babysitting; my daughter has two babysitters and both of them got sick. She was going to have to give her job up and I'm just babysitting to help her out right now. She pays me, but I need to be doing something else. I need to work where I can make a little more money and a few less hours, so I'm going to be looking for something soon.

The lady I sit with, I've been there five years almost and still just make three dollars and fifty cents an hour with her. She's on social security and there's no hope for any advancement or raise in pay or anything. I kind of feel like I'm wasting my time being with her but I hate to quit because I've got five years with her and that kind of helps my record as far as getting other jobs. She does pay social security on me and if the need arises there would be more hours but right now, she's healthy and well and looks good and doesn't need me very much. I feel like I've just kind of reached a dead end right now. I'm at a standstill and I'm not happy.

I do think that things are going to get better. It's like the time my family and I had to spend some time in a spouse abuse shelter in Lexington. My family thought that was terrible, but my kids and I look back on it and we can laugh about it now. My daughters, they didn't want to be there. They put up a sign outside the door that said, "We are hitch-hiking back home. Bye." They wanted to get the message across that they wanted to get back home, but we stayed about three months. The people at the center wanted us to re-locate in Lexington and that would have helped me, but it didn't help my family because that's not what they wanted. I got out and looked for jobs and apartments but I told them I had to come back home. I feel like if we had never had to go to one of those shelters we wouldn't have understood what goes on out there in the world because we saw so much and we thought bad things had only happened to us. We hadn't gone through anything compared to what some of the women and their children there had gone through with. So, it has helped my kids and me. They have compassion now that they might not have had in a lot of situations.

You know, my family has a hard time understanding why my kids and I went through such bad times — you know, why do bad things happen to good people. But I don't look at it that way. I feel like it's just life and you have to make the best of it. That's what we try to do, and I'm sure there will be better days ahead.

(Rebecca has experienced several other family problems with the recent death of her father and her youngest daughter quitting school to get married. She lives alone and continues to work as a sitter with elderly people — a job which she does well.)

ADA

I had a happy childhood growing up. My father was a coal miner and Mom stayed home with the children. She had a birth defect with her eyes and was partially blind. She was a good mother. I had five brothers and two sisters. We had a real good family life and we eight kids had a good time. I laughed a lot with my friends.

We lived on Horse Creek up the little holler called Crawfish. It was a wonderful place — ideal for children to grow up in. You could enjoy yourself. There was a little place up there I called the "bottom." One friend and I would play in the coal tipple and when we would get finished playing, we wouldn't dare to go home we'd be so dirty. We would go up into the "bottom" and there was a spring up behind some trees. It was gorgeous — the trees were like a shower curtain and we would bathe in the creek or in the spring. It was just an ideal place — it was wonderful.

I walked to school about four miles. I went every day and I loved it. It was a pretty big school with a lot of different grades. One reason why we would have to walk so far was us kids decided that we would go over the mountain to get to school, so we always cut across that way and it was the longer way to go. We enjoyed the walking together.

After my sister was born — she was born deaf — my mom moved to Lexington so my sister could get help, and for a short while I went to Lexington to live with Mom. My mom got help through different organizations and she was determined to get my sister an education, which she did as she graduated from high school. I guess we all saw such a need for her to have an education because she was deaf that we really didn't think very much about ourselves.

I went to school in Lexington a year or so until I was in the ninth grade and that's when I quit school and went back to Manchester and was living with my dad and my brothers. I had really done good up until then, but for some reason, I just decided it wasn't worth it any more because there was so much racial things happening and so many fights and so much violence. This was in 1972, then I had a pretty good excuse to quit school — I got married.

My brother-in-law's sister had a party and a cookout. At the time, I wasn't interested in a boyfriend. I walked out on the porch — the dew had fallen on the porch and it was really nice — a wonderful evening. Well, my feet flew out from under me and down I went. This man saw it happen and said, "If you'll come over here, I'll pick you up." I got up — or tried to get up — and fell twice after that. I just crawled off. He laughed. He was real funny — you know, he really enjoyed hisself. He had a good sense of humor.

After that night I started dating him pretty regularly. All I thought of was him. I thought he was the prettiest man in the world. There was nothing or nobody who could be as pretty as he was — strong — perfect, I thought. He was older than me and had already been in the Army. He had come back home and had a job — in fact he still works at the same place.

We got married at my brother-in-law's home. He was a preacher and he married us. It was a nice wedding — small — with the family there. My brother was very dissatisfied, though, and the only thing he would say was "there goes another Saylor girl" — he just couldn't stand for the girls to marry because we'd have to change our name. So I kept my maiden name as well as my married name.

Well, I was sixteen and he was thirty-two. He had already found an apartment because he was living in Hazard at the time. It was everything that I thought it would be to start with. In a way, I expected more, but I was willing to settle because I loved him so good. He was drinking some, but I thought it would get better. From what I understood, from what people told me, it had been worse and he had gotten better, so I thought he would be OK.

He always kept his job. I worked in restaurants waitressing and I worked some at a motel, too. He would tell me that it's all right for me to work but then he would make it really hard on me so I would usually end up missing work and then quit. He was jealous and he wanted me at home and — well, I belonged to him. That's what he really felt and I don't think he ever learned any differently.

After we'd been married about six years our daughter was born. I stayed at home with her and by then my mom had come back from Lexington because my sister had gone on to Danville, Kentucky, to the School for the Deaf and was living in the dorm there. My mom wasn't living too far from me so she helped me with babysitting. Besides working at a restaurant I worked at the Bargain Store and a department store — any place that I could work. These hours was short — they really wasn't big businesses so they couldn't afford to pay much and they would give me small hours.

During this time, my husband still was having a problem with alcohol, in fact, he was getting worse. He certainly wasn't changing for the better. I remember the first time that he really got abusive verbally — made me afraid. We were driving down the road and he told me to light him a cigarette. Well, I was slow and he said, "I said light me a cigarette NOW." I got really scared. That's when I started learning to play peep-eye with his moods — it was like playing a game. I had to play peep-eye with what was going to make him happy.

Then the physical abuse started. I remember the first time was when we were living in Hazard and we had come down to spend a weekend near London and were staying at a motel. He looked at me with his eyes real wild and said, "Who are you?" I looked at him and I said, "You know who I am." He pinned me up against a wall by my throat and even picked me up off the floor it was so severe. He said, "I want to know who you are." I really believe he knew who I was. It scared me terribly bad. Very bad. He eventually just more or less passed out. I was very careful to not arouse any more rage. I was very, very careful. I learned to be very careful to try to make sure he was happy.

For many years, I thought it was all due to alcohol. One reason I stayed in the marriage was because I thought, "Well, someday he'll quit so he'll get better." But I come to realize that it just enhanced his personality. I talked to him about getting help for his drinking but I didn't say very much because I learned how to handle myself around him. I learned the right things to say — the right looks to give him. I learned what kinds of noises to make and not make. So, to ask him to get help, it would just make him very raged because he didn't want to believe he had a problem. I had the problem.

Then after our daughter was born, it got worse for me. I was very protective of her. I remember really bad abuse to me when she was about eight months old. I got out of the house and I went to my mother's and he came over there. He took the baby out of my hands. He knew I'd follow him to the end of the world and drop off as long as he had that baby in his arms. So I went out behind him, and my mom was saying, "Ada, don't go." I said, "He's got my baby." And she knew — she knew that I would follow him. He had my baby.

I was so mixed up at the time of the abuse. I wanted to leave. Then you looked at reality — where were you going to go? To your mother's house? I mean, you gotta go further than that because he'd come and get me.

There was so much mixed feelings. If the abuse wasn't there, he could laugh and he could make you laugh. Or he'd buy you something that was pretty, maybe. If he gave me some kind of a good look — some kind of a good response from him was so good and I was so hungry for that that I was willing to wait around for another good response.

I learned eventually to control things and that would help. You can't stop abuse, you know. It could be maybe the bread wasn't right. He got angry one time because he said I made cornbread without cornmeal. You can't make cornbread without cornmeal. He knew I had made the cornbread with cornmeal. But it's just goes to show how silly it can be. Maybe the table wasn't set right or — just anything. I couldn't make any mistakes because whatever would go wrong would be my fault — my mistake.

About the time my daughter got older and went to school, I had just more or less had to give up. I just stayed home and took care of her while he worked and paid the bills. He did what he wanted to. Far as the money was concerned, I didn't even see his paycheck. He paid the bills and kept things going fairly well. He would go to the grocery store and at the beginning I thought it was because he was doing me a favor. Most women would jump for the chance to have their husband go to the grocery store. But I found out it was because he told me I didn't have enough sense to go — that I would spend too much money. It was something he could control. One time he told me, he said, "I taught you everything you know and you don't know nothing." I said, "Say it again." He said, "I taught you everything you know and you don't know nothing." He kept on saying it and I said, "You taught me everything you know and I don't know nothing." And he finally got it. He caught on to what he was a-saying. And it was true. He had taught me everything he knowed. He had me well trained.

Christmas before last, the day after Christmas was probably the worst time of it. He had been drinking — you know, the holidays was always really bad. He was just raging and he had backed me up into the kitchen and I really thought he was going to kill me. My daughter was running. I had told her, "Always run. Always run away, don't never intervene. Run — no matter what you hear, no matter what you see — run. Don't try to help me, run." I taught her to do that and I taught her to go to the car and to lay down in the seat, or in the floor.

Well, he had backed me up against the wall in the kitchen and I really thought that he would kill me. I was trying to find something to kill him first. He had broken a chair and I was trying to feel around. He had me pinned in by the throat. I was trying to find a weapon and I was feeling around on the counter and the stove for a knife, for anything. Then I came to myself and I realized, he would die or I would die.

I finally got away. I had gotten a phone number of a safe house off the wall at Kentucky Fried Chicken. I had written it down and kept it so long that I knew the number. I had kept it for years. I used it to call and I asked them, what should I do, and they told me to go to the city police station.

I took my daughter to a friend's house. She was very scared but I didn't know what to expect at the safe house. I didn't know what would be there, so I took her to a friend's house. It was so cold — it was bitterly cold. I walked down at the river. I watched the river run down behind the city police and I thought, boy, if I was on that water I would go and go and I'd just keep a-going. It was so free, the water was moving so free — it was what I wanted to do. I wanted to be like the water.

Well, when I first went in the police station, they told me, they said, "We'll have to call the safe house and see if they've got room." I had to explain to them that I had already called and I was just needing them to escort me. One of the city policemen said, "You know, some women like this." — and there I was, beat to the point that I couldn't hardly walk up the steps. I mean, I was barely walking. They escorted me on to the safe house and then I went from there to the hospital. I didn't have broken bones that time — my kidneys was bruised. He learned where to put the bruises. He learned that it was less noticeable to beat my head against the car window than it was to beat my face with his fist and he learned that nobody else was going to see my body. He knew where to put the bruises — he learned. He knew.

Unfortunately, he had a friend that had a girl friend that called around to places for him. She suspected that being beat that I would go to the safe house. She called the hospital and the hospital unfortunately gave out the information that I had been there and had been treated for abuse. So she called the safe house and I talked to her. I convinced her not to tell him that I was at the safe house. The next day I got my daughter from my friend and she stayed with me.

I had a court date coming up to have a restraint order on him. It took me two weeks to get my nerve up to do that because I was afraid. I was afraid of anything and everybody, really. I didn't trust nobody. You know, you don't trust, you learn that. I mean, if somebody loves you, if they are not good to you, then why is people going to be good to you that don't know you?

The day I went to get the restraint order there was a couple inside the courtroom and the man pulled a gun. All the policemen and everybody was running here and there and I thought, here I am, running from a man and there's a man in here with a gun. I went and got under the desk. I thought, I'm having to fight for my life here, too. I was so scared.

When I went to the safe house they knew I was completely

numb. There wasn't any tears, there wasn't nothing. I was empty. They gave me the opportunity if I wanted to talk and if I didn't, okay. They showed me that if you want to, you can work your way out. They helped me to know that it takes time to heal — to heal both mentally and physically. They offered me counseling but I wasn't ready for it. You're not always ready for it. I wasn't at that time. It's a scary thing for them, too, because they're working with you and this man that you're running from considered you his. He considers them messing with his life and it puts them in danger.

I got the restraining order finally, after I had been at the safe house two months. We went to court and then I went back to him. I thought I would try again, but the abuse started happening again. It was like a cycle. It would get better. He was still on the restraining order — I could live with him but he couldn't beat me. He was on the restraint a year, and the very week it lifted he was very verbally abusive and then he got physically abusive, too. He would tie a wet towel around my neck — things like that. Then in February, he had a big blowup. I had been gone and came in and sat down in a chair and when I looked at him I knew that he would kill me. I made my mind up then — I went out the door and I never went back. I went back to the safe house. There they said, "Ada, don't worry, because some women — they'll leave two or three times before they get strong enough." But, I was strong enough this time.

I stayed just a few days and then they helped me find a place to live. At first he would call me a lot and ask me out or sometimes he tried to threaten me. Then after that didn't work because I kept my distance from him, he told me how cruel the world was. He knew I was naive, that I had never been out in the world. I don't know that much about it and he knows that. I mean, who would know it better than him? He raised me — he knows me well.

We live about thirty-five miles apart now. I've moved and I don't think he knows where my new apartment is. He's still drinking because he's been picked up for DUI. He's never gone to get help. I went to Al-Anon. The first night that I went I was just getting over a beating. I was getting desperate — I knew I had to survive for my child — I knew I had to make it for her. My daughter loves her dad but she knew how things were. The night I had to leave she said, "I've had about as much as I can take and Mommy, I know you have." She knew things had to change and she's accepted it. His mother, she knew about the abuse and she would just say, "Ada, take care of him if you can." They knew the situation and they don't blame me. I don't talk to them because it wouldn't be fair to put them in a position like that.

I had worked on my GED three times while I was still with him, but he would make it so hard that I would just give up. Then I began to do it secretly and when I went into the safe house, I was well into working on my GED secretly. I went in the daytime. I had a lot of books, the GED workbooks that they let me bring home to work on. While I worked on my GED at the Community College they also let me take an English class that I got college credit for.

While I was working on my GED, I had so many things on my mind. I had so much to deal with — so many problems, that it was draining me. I wasn't stupid. I could learn. After I started taking the English class, it really encouraged me tremendously. The teacher, she was so excited when she heard that I passed my GED — she heard before I did. When I went to class I sat down and my teacher said, "You've got it." I was jumping up and down and everybody else was too. I had so many people rooting for me. I was separated by then, I was finishing the college class in which I made an "A" and then immediately after class was out I came to the New Opportunity School.

I was scared to come to the New Opportunity School, but I was so thirsty for knowledge I just felt like a sponge, needing to just soak it up. I know now that knowledge and education is for me. I didn't really realize my potential until I came to the New Opportunity School. It was hard — after so many years of being told that you are stupid and you can't do nothing right and you'll never amount to anything. You build these things up over years and you don't get them out in a day or two. When I came to Berea, I met people like Wilma Dykeman, Gurney Norman, the Stephensons — people that believed in me — let me know that I could expand. For years I felt like I was in a little box and I would walk right around in that little box. Every now and then I'd see light but since I have been on my own I have seen tremendous doors opened. People that know me say, "Ada, this is unreal. Everything is opening up for you." I felt like I got out from under a curse.

I am drawing AFDC and I get food stamps. I house clean for people. Things has worked out by miracles. I've paid my rent — never failed one time paying it. I've paid my bills — all of them. Things has worked out and eventually, I'll get a good job.

When I go to school this fall I'll go full-time so I can have some help financially — I can stay on AFDC while in school. Of course, my husband has never contributed to anything that would benefit me. When my divorce becomes final they are strict with the father paying child support while I'm drawing AFDC.

I feel very good about myself. I feel real strong. I know there's going to be a lot of things, a lot of obstacles in the way, but gee, look what I've overcome already.

I would say to other women in my situation to do the best that you can do. Maybe you don't see no way out. But as long as you keep on a-pushing and working on yourself, eventually you will see a way out. Eventually you will see a light. Some people who go through something like this, they indulge themselves and maybe get into drinking problems theirselves. Or maybe they start taking pills — but that don't make them a bad person, it just made a way of escape for them. My escape was music, music and books. Sometimes at night I would play the piano and I would look up and it would be daylight and I wouldn't even know it. That was what I needed. Everybody has to have an escape. The thought came to my mind sometimes that if you can't beat 'em, join 'em. I'm strong, but I didn't know it at first. See, I had that strength in there — it just kept a-rolling around and around, but I didn't know I had it. I was fortunate.

I'm happy. For the first time in so long I don't have fears. I'm thirty-seven years old. From the time I was sixteen years old I had dealt with abuse — until now. And now I'm just really getting my own feelings.

When I had just got my GED I said, "Alright, I'm going to take four more years just to concentrate on getting an education." I'd like to major in education. I'd like to be able to teach. Or maybe I'd like to write. I'd like to tell people my story if it could maybe help somebody. I've got some stories to tell that are not so good, but maybe they'd help somebody else. I definitely want to help other people.

(Ada is currently enrolled full-time in a Community College near her home. She plans to transfer to Berea College after her daughter finishes high school. Her dream is that her daughter will be able to come to Berea College at the same time she transfers. Ada has given several talks to groups across Kentucky to tell people her story and she was recently featured in WOMEN'S WORLD magazine.)

BEA

I was born at home in August of 1944 in the little community of Roan Mountain, Tennessee. My father walked to town and got the doctor and brought him back to the house. I was born in the same house and community where all my ancestors came from. Originally all this land was my great-grand-father's who had three wives and lots of children. He divided the land up between the children then it passed on down through the heirs on my father's side of the family. My mom was from about ten miles north of Roan Mountain in a community called Elk Creek. Now that's where all the Florida people go to and have bought up so much of the property there. The Florida people, they began to come in when my mother was young. In fact, my mother was practically raised by a couple from Florida. My mother's mother died when she was about twelve years old, then when my mother was about thirteen, this Florida couple took her in and she did housekeeping and had a place to live. They would take her to Florida with them so she got to travel quite a bit that way. They called her their adopted daughter, and we were close to them all of our lives.

But Daddy's people were all from Roan Mountain and that's where I grew up. I was the first child. I don't know how long we lived in the house where I was born, but we moved from there down to a place we called "the holler" which is right above my father's homeplace. We lived there probably two or three years and my earliest childhood memory is when we lived in the holler. That's when my baby brother was born and I've got a sister that's younger than him.

Daddy did a lot of carpentry work. I followed him every step he took, and he called me his little shadow. I was with my father constantly, so Daddy was the one who taught me many nursery rhymes. We didn't have books, but Daddy knew these nursery rhymes. He taught me things like "Jack be nimble, Jack be quick." And he had a candle that he put on the old, rough wooden floors and we made a game of it. He'd have me jump over it. And he would tell me stories about the Three Bears and Little Red Riding Hood. I was his companion, I guess, when I was just a toddler — about two or three years old. Daddy liked to farm also.

When I was very young I was taught that I couldn't hit anyone or fight or anything, no matter what they did. I had a cousin who terrorized me by biting me, and this went on for some time. Finally, one day, my relatives had been visiting us and after they left, my mother, she saw teeth marks on my back where my cousin had bit me. She showed my back to Daddy and he got real upset. He told me that from now on, I was allowed to hit back. I couldn't start a fight, but I was to take my part. So, the next time the relatives came over to visit, he bit me again and when he did, I bit the fire out of his arm, just took a big chunk out. He never gave me any trouble after that.

Roan Mountain was a community that could survive on its own. It had a country store and the post office was in the store. There was also a hardware store, a band mill, a chair factory, a grist mill, and a big, two-story boarding house. Most of these things were in the head of the creek, where it is very mountainous. The rest of the community is more like a valley where all the homes are and everything. But, the community could more or less survive on its own.

There was a school there. In fact, my great-grandfather is the one who donated the land and more than likely he is the one that built the building. He started the church there and he also started the First Baptist Church in a nearby town. But in Roan Mountain, this little frame building was first a schoolhouse and then they started having church services in it. My father went to school in this building and when I was a child we held church services there. It was a big building with an upstairs to it.

We moved from the holler and went up to Shell Creek and lived with my Grandpa Smith — my mother's father. I had to walk down off the top of a big mountain to catch the school bus. I started to school at Shell Creek and went to that school for a couple of years then we moved back to Roan Mountain and I went to school there. We kind of switched back and forth between the two communities until I was about thirteen. That's when we made the final move. There was a place that had belonged to an aunt and they had bought property away from the home place and built them a new house, so when they left we moved into their place and this is where my mother is living to this day.

Late in his life, my father began working in some of the factories in Elizabethton, about fifteen miles from Roan Mountain. He would catch rides with someone. We didn't have an automobile.

Daddy started drinking. He may have drunk all his life. I don't know. But anyway, as I got older, his drinking got worse. And when he would drink, it would change him completely. The family doctor told us that for him to take a drink of alcohol was like drinking poison. But he loved to drink — and he would go on those binges. It caused us to have to do without a lot. It caused us to have to suffer a lot. He would work, but he would take a whole week's pay and drink on the weekend. It would go for drink and we would have to do without.

My mother never worked on a public job until after my sister left home. I think it was after she graduated from high school that mother started working at the hospital doing housekeeping — it's the only public job that she's ever had. She wanted to get jobs, but it would scare her to have to go take a test or something. She just blanked out, and I do the same thing now. It would scare her to death.

I think Mother and Daddy both went to about the eighth grade. Daddy was considered by many in the community to be like a genius with intelligence. He had so much common sense and was so smart and he hadn't been taught. I remember when people were at the house at his funeral there was different people that was referring to him as a genius. But, alcohol just ruled his life for so many years. I grew up thinking that I hated my daddy because of the suffering, because when he'd get drunk, he would beat my mother. It was my job to protect Mother because I was the oldest and for some reason, if one of us kids was around, Daddy wouldn't hit Mother. I can remember dreading Friday evenings and wondering if Daddy would be drunk. If he was drinking, I'd have to stick close to Mother. I mean, I would be out of sight, but I had to watch their every move.

One time when I was about twelve, it was one Friday and Daddy was drunk so I went in another room where I could hear. I heard the outside door close, so I knew he'd taken her out — to get her away from the house where he could beat on her. So I went running through the house and went to the kitchen and looked out the window where I could see them and I saw them going down through the garden towards the barn. So, I went out on the back porch and watched and when they went in the barn, I went running down through the field. When I got to the barn, I called, "Mother." I checked all the barn stalls on the ground floor and kept calling Mother's name. It was stone quiet. No sound at all. I knew they were in that barn, so I kept searching. I started going up the stairs to the barn loft — still calling Mother's name. No response. When I got to the top of the steps of the barn loft, I saw Mother laying on her back and Daddy was sitting straddle of her with his hands around her neck. I started crying and screaming at Daddy asking him what he was doing to my mother. He just got up and he left, and, of course, I was real upset. Mother was just shaking all over, and she told me that he told her if she said a word, he'd choke her to death, so she couldn't respond. I know that's one time he would've killed her if I hadn't been there. There was several times that things like that happened.

My mother loved him, but she couldn't take the abuse. She left him several times, because she had to. It was when he was drinking that she would go stay with her sister or a relative for three or four days until he got sober. My brother and sister and I would stay at the house. As soon as she'd leave, Daddy would quit drinking and he would take care of us. Mother knew he would do that but she must have really worried about us. But it would be like she would have to escape from him or something, so she didn't have time to get us or anything like that. One time she climbed an apple tree. We had a big apple orchard and she climbed up in a tree and hid from him that way. That was when my sister was a baby. It was after dark and we was all in the bed. Mother got out of the house away from him, and I'd heard him hollering at her. After she got out of the house, he passed out. I slipped out of bed and went to the living room and saw him laying there and I went out on the porch and started hollering for Mother. In a few minutes she came creeping up to the edge of the porch and wanted to know if Daddy was asleep. I told her "yes." and she told me she had been hiding in a tree.

I never worried that he would start beating on us, but he was stricter with me than with my brother and my sister. By the time our sister was born — she is nine years younger than me — he was a lot different with her than with us. It was important to him that we have manners and that we made good in school, really important that we were perfect. It seems like the harder we tried, the more he disapproved — there was no way to please him. I don't know if it was the alcohol or what, but anyway, I grew up thinking I hated my daddy and I loved my mother because she went through so much. But later when my husband and I married and moved to Roan Mountain with our sons I feel like it was meant to be because I got real close to Daddy. He apologized. He had stopped drinking by then, and saw where he had done wrong and he suffered. It about killed him when he got older because he couldn't stand the thoughts of what he had done. I've heard my grandparents — his mother and daddy — I've heard them say how different Daddy was from the rest of the children. They were just normal, but Daddy was always different. He would speak above other people's level. I feel my grandparents didn't realize the potential of what Daddy could do and he wasn't guided in the right direction — if he had just been encouraged to get an education. Whenever he would say or do something that was really intelligent or different, he was made fun of and belittled. If he wanted to do something that was out of the ordinary or if he thought of something out of the ordinary, they made fun of him. They didn't realize what they were doing. And his frustration caused him to drink and then the alcohol caused him to behave in the way he did and it was sort of like a cycle with him then.

I look back and think — boy, I was really fortunate to have parents that didn't teach me that it was bad luck to do this or that — they didn't teach me superstitions, and to think of my father back in those days teaching me those nursery rhymes. That showed that he loved me and he wanted me to learn. I just can't imagine a father doing that. Usually men don't do those things.

My parents really encouraged me to stay in school but college was never mentioned. I have wondered why no one ever mentioned college to me. It was like something like that was just a different world and we was so poor that we didn't dare to consider it. But then I've wondered why the teachers didn't talk to me because I did real good in school. Then, when I was in the eleventh grade, I got married. Maybe it was because I got married that the teachers didn't mention college. But I went on and finished high school and made real good grades.

I was married for four years and I didn't know what love was. You know, I was just a kid. It was a big thing for me to go on to finish high school. I went to school a year and a half married and people made fun of me because I was married and going on to high school, but I wouldn't have even considered dropping out. After I finished high school I went to work in a sewing factory over in Elizabethton. This was about the only kind of work that women could do, because there was not that much industry.

I think I married to get away from Daddy. He was drinking and life at home was terrible — just terrible. I found this to be a good way to escape. I married a person from about ten miles from us — a cousin of mine introduced us. We had a pretty good marriage but I think that I outgrew him or something. I just decided that I didn't want to be married to him any more.

After I divorced him I came up to Kentucky with a cousin. I was living in London with two women, sharing an apartment and my cousin kept wanting me to meet a man they worked with. They said we were so much alike but I wasn't interested in meeting anybody. Anyway, they finally slipped him over to our apartment one evening and they wanted us to go out to dinner. I told them I had plans with a girlfriend — we were going to see "Mary Poppins." Lord, that's been so many years. I remember that was when "Mary

Poppins" had just come out and we wanted to see that movie so I left all of them sitting in the apartment and went on to get my friends. We went to the movie and came back and there they were still waiting for me. They had been playing cards and had stayed at the apartment waiting for me to come back. So anyway, after I got acquainted with Jacob and all, I found out that he wasn't so bad after all.

When I moved to London I got a job over at a factory and worked in the shipping department where I learned all of the compounds for the stock room and pulled orders and worked with IBM cards. I didn't want to go back to Tennessee. I knew if I did Mother would want me going back to my former husband because she didn't believe in divorce. Once while I was married I left him and went to Mother's and Daddy's and Mother went and called him and told him I was there. She thought I was too young to know what I was doing. Those were kind of rough times. I wanted a new life, but I ended up in the hospital. I had a sinus infection and I was real nervous. When I was in there, I talked to my doctor about my problems and about me trying to leave my husband. I wasn't happy. He said, "Isn't there somebody in your family that you can go and live with for awhile to give you time to get back on your feet?" I told him there wasn't. That I didn't want to impose on anybody — and also because I knew that I had already been home to Mother's once and I got sent back. So, I thought, well, the only thing I can do is just run away. And that's what I did.

After I got up to London I called Mother and Daddy and told them where I was at. I had left without telling them good bye or telling them where I was going. That was a big shocker — that I would do this terrible thing. I had just turned twenty-one and hadn't been anywhere very much. I think the farthest I had been was to Georgia, when we went there somewhere to some relative's funeral. But I knew that I wasn't going to stay in that mess any more. I just wanted out. I think those decisions helped me be more understanding with my own boys.

It was so hard on me during those days. I thought if I ever have a family that my children are going to know that I love them and they are going to be welcome. If there's anything I can do for them, I'll do it. I will not take up for the in-law. But — my parents didn't really know my circumstances. I didn't talk, I didn't tell them. They thought I was just wanting to leave for no reason.

After coming to Kentucky, my life was so different. It was just like going from hell to heaven. It was. I enjoyed life — it was so different — it was fun to be alive. The very first place I went to, I got a job. And, I started saving my money. It was just like — well, everything fell in place.

Then I met Jacob and it seemed like that every time I needed to do anything, he was there to help. It started out kind of like a friendship. I was really brushing him off — resisting his friendship, but then it kind of blossomed. I have wondered, you know they talk about things in your life that's meant to be.

We had been going together six months when Jacob and I got married. We got married in London. We had planned on getting married in his home church in Corbin, but Jacob was working for a company that had started laying off and he got laid off from work so I started trying to help him with his bills. So all this money I'd saved up for my wedding — it began to dwindle. When we started out it was really tough. And then he decided he was going to change jobs. That's when he got a job as a fireman. He loved it.

I worked for a while but after I got pregnant with Bill I started having female problems. I started spotting and we was afraid I was going to lose the baby so I quit my job. Jacob was working a good job then, so I quit my job and was careful about not being on my feet and I had to rest every now and then. When I was pregnant with Joe I had to be real careful too. He was born three years later, and I stayed home with the kids all during that time.

We moved down to Raleigh, North Carolina, after Joe was born. We would live somewhere about two or three years and Jacob would get to wanting to move to some other town — I guess he likes to travel. Anyway, I didn't know that then. He had wanted to go to California — I told him I'd never live in California because of earthquakes. Then he checked on the Washington, D.C., area and the crime rate was so tremendous and the expenses were so much higher that he quickly ruled that out. He decided he wanted to go to Raleigh. I had nothing to do with his decision to go to Raleigh other than I said I wasn't going to live in California. He went to school there for about three years while he was working at the fire department — he was taking computer courses and things like that.

He liked working for the fire department but he came very close to getting killed about three times. And each time something like that happened, it would just tear me all to pieces. I thought I was going to have to raise the children by myself, so, I started begging him to quit. The educational system in the area we lived in was not the best — a lot of problems, a lot of racial problems. And with him working at the fire department he heard all this — he heard about teachers that would get cut up with knives. The students would be carrying them in the classrooms. Things like that. He'd say, "Honey, we'll have to get the children out of here — we've got to get them away from here." He didn't want them going to school there.

When Joe went to kindergarten I started working. I worked in a corrugated container company — a company making cardboard boxes but we weren't allowed to call it that — it had to be corrugated containers. I made real good money, but it was very heavy work. In fact, there was only five women employed in the factory. The rest of them were men so it was very strenuous work, but I hung in there on account of the pay.

For years Jacob had talked about moving to my home town in the mountains. He loved it there and wanted to live there where my family showered attention and love on him. Unfortunately, his family isn't close, so he had never known anything like that kind of attention other than from my family. And we were always having family picnics and get togethers and things. Every time he would mention us moving up there, I would tell him there wasn't any way to make a living. I had been working at the corrugated container company for some time and conditions were getting worse and worse at work. I was beginning to break down. I was having a lot of female problems and of the women that worked there, every one had hysterectomies. One day at lunch time, I had just had it. I went home and when I got home, Jacob was there. He had taken the day off for some reason. I started crying and I said, "I just can't take it any more. I cannot hold up any longer." I said I was in pain from lifting them big, heavy boxes and things. He said, "All right, now's a good time for us to go to the mountains." So I didn't go back to the factory. He went to the fire department and told them we were going to move to the mountains. Oh, they had a fit. His captain talked to me, tried to get me to get Jacob to change his mind and when we left, the captain told him, he said, "I'll give you two years at the most and you'll be back." But he hasn't gone back to it.

So we moved back to my home community about five hundred feet from my parents and my kids went to school right there where I had gone to school. They were growing up in the same community and went to the same church. My sister's husband told Jacob that they were hiring where he was working at a factory. He had been working at this factory for years and knew he could get him on. Sure enough, Jacob got on there, but, he had been working only about three weeks and they started having all this lay-off because the economy started going down. Many places were closing and shutting down.

I went to work in the sewing factory again for four years. Then they closed, and Jacob was out of work for a long time. He got a job in another factory and they began the lay-offs too. It was just like that he couldn't get a job hardly, and when he got a job there would be something would happen. It was really rough — very, very hard. We had close to ten years of very hard years when we stayed in the Tennessee mountains.

Well, Jacob wasn't finding work and his mother was calling him, talking about her health — how bad it was, that she was ready for a wheel-chair. He was really worried about her and of course, I was concerned, too. His parents had divorced when he was real little. His father is still alive and lives in Corbin. Well, his mother was in better health than me. I'll put it this way, she'll outlive me a long time — she wasn't ready for any wheelchair. But Jacob came up here and got a job driving tractor trailers — long haul driving.

I stayed on in Tennessee taking care of the garden and canning. He stayed with his mom for a couple of weeks, then he found a place for us in Winchester. We lived down on Main Street — close to the Baptist Church. We rented a little house down there that was so tiny that we had to store a lot of our furniture in my mother's attic and his mother's basement.

The boys started to high school in Winchester. We spent two to three years looking for another place to rent before we finally found one out in the country. When we moved out in the country, we drove the boys to school so they could stay in the school in town. I liked the school, the teachers, and everything, and felt like they could learn more there.

Life was very difficult for me. It had been difficult for the boys ever since we had gone back to the mountains to my people. I hadn't really wanted to go back there to start with but after we moved and I got back into the family and got roots settled down there, I didn't want to leave. I was getting older, too. Factories were beginning to come into the mountains, so I felt like my husband could get a good job there and that I could, too. But Jacob felt his heartstrings tugging him up here towards his mother because of the things she would tell him over the phone — how bad off she was. So he wanted us to come up here to help take care of her.

Jacob would be gone all week — came home only on the weekends. He very, very seldom would see or even talk to his mother. This is the irony of it. Here Bill and Joe and myself were in this strange town with no family — his family doesn't visit. It felt to us like we had just been dumped in a strange town with no communication with people. It was very hard.

It didn't take the boys long to find friends and everything. But they still felt hurt — it did damage, just the fact that our lives were torn up. When we found this place out in the country, I told Jacob, I said, "I'm tired of moving now. I'm just too old. From now on," I said, "When I move from this place here, unless it's a place that we bought, the furnishing will go to my mother's because I'm not moving any more." I guess he knows that I mean it because I'm sure he would be wanting us to move to Lexington where he's working now. Someone asked him why we didn't move to Lexington and he looked over at me and he said, "Bea won't leave Winchester." They looked at me real hard and I said, "That's right. I am not leaving here and when I do leave, it'll be for my mother's." I am not moving to another town. He is the one who chose to work in Lexington — that's his choice and he can drive it. I tried to get him to get a job here in Winchester. He wanted to work with horses so that was his decision. And if that's what he wants to do, that's fine with me as long as we're not moving.

Ever since we moved here I haven't had a job. I spent my time taking the children to school and waiting for them, taking them to band practice and play practice. They were both very active, and I was busy with them and Jacob was on the road gone all the time. But I was so busy with Bill and Joe that it seemed like the time would go by real fast, but the boys were wishing they were back home with their friends in Tennessee.

Then Jacob fell and broke his arm. He broke both the big bones in his arm and couldn't change gears. They tell me, though, that they're putting automatic transmissions in a lot of those trucks now. But anyway, he had to stop driving. He had had trouble with his back while we were in Tennessee, and he had surgery on it three times. So there was about three years that he wasn't able to work when we were having it so hard back in Tennessee. After we moved up here and he started driving the truck he made real good money, but then he fell and broke his arm and here he was, out of work again.

I had just started to feel a little comfortable. For a long time I had been afraid something would happen that we wouldn't have that income and then all of a sudden — bam — it did happen. I mean, this was at a time I was beginning to relax and kind of enjoy life a little. Then, it was back on us again. He was out of work about two years because something happened to his arm. I think the doctor called it sympathetic nerve syndrome. His arm would swell, and it did this for over a year. He went to a bone doctor, then a specialist at the University. They tried different things to keep that arm from swelling like that, but his hand would swell up like he has been bee-stung or something. But the specialist at the University told him he had seen some people's arm or leg do this for as long as two years. Then all of a sudden it quit and they don't know why.

This was about the time I heard about and decided to apply to the New Opportunity School. We had gone to Hardee's one Sunday and there was a Sunday paper there with a big color picture of a woman who had gone to the New Opportunity School at Berea College. There was no doubt in my mind that it was the answer to my prayers. My boys were both going to be gone away from home to school. They had encouraged me to check into going to school so when I saw the write-up in the paper about the New Opportunity School, I thought, wow, this is a chance of a lifetime! So I sent my application off. Bill called me and I said, "Now don't tell anyone in the family — this can't be told because I may not be chosen." I said, "I'm sure that there's younger women and more than likely they'll choose these women that have young children because they'll think that they need the help more so than me because my children are grown." Bill said, "Now Mom, calm down. You've got just as good a chance as anybody else. Now don't start looking at the down side of it." I think he told me that he wouldn't tell anybody about it. Well, a few days later, my mother called and she was wanting to know about me going to Berea College. Bill had let it slip to her. I said, "No, Mother, there's nothing that's happened yet." Then, when I was accepted I was so happy. So happy. I just couldn't believe it. It still just seems unreal.

When I came to the New Opportunity School and started looking into going to Berea College I realized then that I could go without it costing a whole lot. That was a wonderful surprise. I knew this was the answer to my prayer. I feel like that these things happen — like a lot of times there is someone that has control of our lives more than we realize.

So after I finished the New Opportunity School I enrolled in one class at Berea College. I took English Composition. Meanwhile Joe was planning on going to college at Eastern Kentucky University. So we started together the same year as freshmen — I had two sons in college and I was in college.

I don't think Jacob believed it would last long. I think he thought I would get tired of it. He encouraged me but later, he did come to mind. Before I started school I had gone around to different factories and tried to get a job. Some of the places wouldn't even take an application, so I had told him that after I went to school for a little while then I could get a better paying job and be able to help more. So Jacob was very supportive and I think he thought that maybe this would last a semester or so but then I decided I wanted to try going full-time. I didn't have time for cooking or cleaning or doing any of the family things. I about made myself sick. But I thought that if I could go full-time I could get my education over with so quick and then I could be out in the work field. But I didn't stop to realize that this might be at the expense of my marriage breaking up or something. I came to the realization that there wasn't any rush for this education and that I could take my time and that it would be better to take my time and enjoy going to school and make better grades and be able to take care of my family.

Meanwhile Jacob got a different job in Lexington, but this past winter he kind of put pressure on me, wanting me to quit. I had a conference with the Dean and I said, "This is the first time in my life that I've had anything done for me." I told him that my husband was putting pressure on me to quit in order for me to go to work and it was causing a lot of problems. The Dean told me, he said that he felt like I should do it for me — that I should continue my school for myself. If I could hang in there about four and a half more years then I would be able to make so much more money. When I left his office, I knew I wasn't going to quit. I knew that if it meant giving up my marriage, then I would.

From about the first of December until recently, Jacob wouldn't even speak to me. I have never gone through anything like this with him before in our marriage. At Christmas time, he didn't even get me a Christmas card. We've always gotten each other at least a card, if we couldn't afford anything else. And I've saved them — that's part of our Christmas decorations. Joe couldn't understand why his dad was doing this. Well, he had just quit talking — it was as though I wasn't in the room. If he did say something, he'd say it to Joe about me. It would be real hateful or smart aleck, so Joe asked him why he was doing this. I mean, it was just so different for him — it was out of character for him. Jacob told him that there was things going on that he didn't know about. Joe and I tried to figure out what those things were, but we couldn't figure it out. He must have been thinking about the bills or something. But, he did tell Joe that he had had to wash a load of clothes for himself, and there was one weekend I had been busy doing something and he had to cook himself a steak or something. Well, he thought that was terrible. So Joe asked him, "Well, Daddy, couldn't you do that? What did it hurt you to do that?"

Well, he had told Joe I was going to have to leave. Joe said, "Dad, Mom's not leaving. If anyone leaves, it'll be you." Jacob doesn't know I know about all these conversations. But Joe said, "Mom, if he wants to go and live with Ma-maw, I'll help you. We'll pay the rent and I'll stay here and help you. Don't you worry about it." He would not hear of me dropping out.

I stood my ground and finally one day about three weeks ago, I was in the kitchen doing dishes and Jacob said, "How much longer are you going to be going to school?" I said, "Well, if I'm lucky, if I hang in there, about four and a half more years." He said, "What?" I said, "Well, I know this one woman that it took eight years." I said, "This is nothing unusual." He wanted to know why in the world I had to take a World Religions course, why I would take courses that don't help me. I told him, I said, "Well, Jacob, that course helped. It's just that you have to take other subjects besides what you major in. I have to have twenty-three subjects besides my major." Well, we talked for about twenty minutes and since then he's been all right. I'm glad I stood my ground now, but there for awhile it looked like that there wasn't going to be a marriage. This is the first time this has happened in our marriage because I have always given in to him. This is the first and only time I've done this.

Jacob has got his side, too, you know. It's hard. I mean, for a couple of years we had to try to make do with one vehicle. And he did go out and buy me a car — went in debt for it so I could get to college.

Well, I have seen this thing that has happened between Jacob and me as a big turning point in our life for him more so than me. I think it was an acceptance to him that I am going to go ahead and get my education. I would love for us to be able to stay here and me work with women who are having a hard time raising their children — something similar to social work. I'd like to have my degree probably in Sociology and minoring in Appalachian Studies. Seems like if you can understand something from every point that you can be a better person. I think one of the biggest decisions women have to make is right at the beginning when they leave their family and go to the New Opportunity School and if they can make that decision, that's critical for them.

When I was in the New Opportunity School, everything contributed toward the whole — every one of the seminars. It helped me very, very much. In fact, I would like to go back and attend a class or two and get a little boost. Gurney Norman's writing class helped as he encouraged us to write our feelings and when he complimented my writing it made me feel like I can do something. And writing a resume — that helped me see that the things I had done were important toward getting a job. And at the school it was the first time I had ever heard of Appalachian Literature in my life, and that just opened up a new world for me. This semester I am taking Appalachian Literature because I have wanted to take this course ever since I came to Berea College. It makes me feel kind of guilty to get college credit for something that is so much fun. I start reading and I don't want to stop; I want to read all night long. It's just wonderful!

I want every woman to know that there is a chance for her — that they all can take that big step toward changing their lives. It's so critical for them to get encouragement, and it is so important for them if they can just take that big step. I have changed so much that my children get tickled at me and they'll say, "That's the way to go, Mom!"

(Bea eventually had to quit school at Berea College as her husband took a job in another state. Recently they moved back to Kentucky and Bea has a good secretarial job at a state university and has plans to continue her education part-time there. Both boys are married and working on advanced degrees.)

BEVERLY

I grew up spending my time between Kentucky and Tennessee. I'm the oldest child of three. My dad attended the University of Tennessee. He worked his way through college — he would go out west and work the wheat harvest in the summers and in the fall come back and go to school. He left home at sixteen. He was a depression-age child and got farmed out a lot but finally ended up working his way through school. We moved around a lot because he was looking for a job. That's why we ended up in several little places in Tennessee and then finally came to Kentucky when he got a job as an engineer. Dad grew up in Tennessee, but my mom was from McCreary County in Kentucky. She was born there — my family goes back four generations there. When I was a child my great-grandmother was still living and I stayed with my grandparents a lot.

My grandmother was a forward woman for her time because she farmed; she wasn't a housekeeper. I'm afraid I took after her. My great-grandmother did the housekeeping. I can remember her getting up at four in the morning. She cooked on a wood cookstove. She wouldn't use electric and she'd bring you out of bed with the smell of biscuits — I mean, breakfast at that time was the main meal of the day. She fixed everything to eat. Then my grandmother and I would head out to the cornfield where we would manage to stay most of the day. Summers were always spent with my grandparents — but I would go back home to go to school.

The first two years I was in school I went to a school in Tennessee that was condemned when I went there — two years ago they finally built a new school. We moved back to Kentucky when I was in fifth grade because my dad had got a job and my mother had attended beautician school; she became a self-employed beautician, working out of our house.

We bought a farm about a half a mile from my grandparents where I had spent all those summers. The house had no running water, and had outside bathrooms, which was an experience to say the least. After several renovations, Mom finally put a shop in. Then she became pregnant with my brother. About a year and a half after he was born she had what would be the equivalent of a nervous breakdown. She had to quit doing hair.

I was the oldest child and it didn't matter if I was a boy or a girl — we all worked on the farm. Nowadays you would say we was poor, but we didn't know it. At that time, I thought I was the richest person in the world. I had all that land to roam around on and I loved it. I loved to farm; I have been doing it since I was a small child. I always had calves to feed every morning before I went to school and that was back when we had the old time bucket feeders and you got milk splashed everywhere all over you. Then when my mother became sick I had most of the housework to do and my brother to see to. I was eleven when I started taking care of him.

When we first moved back to Kentucky, I had to walk about a quarter of a mile out to a neighbor's house to catch the bus every morning. They didn't have a bus route on the road I lived on. I'd have to get up and feed the animals, then get ready and take off for school.

I went to school to please my dad because you didn't cross Daddy. If he told you to go, you went. He didn't ever hold us out of school to work on the farm — he wasn't that type. He believed in making sure that you went to school. I didn't enjoy going to school — it was just a necessity I had to do. I could never see anything else I wanted to do but farm.

I come from a highly destructional family in the respect that we were taught not to show emotion. We were not allowed to cry. I remember my grandmother died in 1959, which was my dad's mama, and nobody shed a tear in the whole family. I mean, this was just the way it was — you were weak or defective if you showed any type of emotion. My mother's people were more emotional but when she had her nervous breakdown, nobody understood it and that really prevented her from getting the proper help she needed at that time. You know, the doctors just kept her on nerve pills and there was no really adequate care given to her.

I started drinking when I was fourteen. We had a neighbor that I was pretty close to; her son and I was pretty close also and booze was always around — readily available at their house. When I started drinking, my family was not aware of it at all. The drinking was controlled to the point to where I knew what I could get away with and it wasn't that frequent. Mother was working again by then and Daddy was working, and as long as I had the house cleaned and supper cooked, nobody really paid that much attention to what was going on.

Going to my neighbor's house to drink was the only form of release I had. I wasn't allowed to release at home. I was always the responsible child — I was born the responsible child. I was always responsible for what everybody else did. I had nobody that I could talk to so drinking was the only form of release I had. It was a crazy time, now that I look back. There was just a lot happening.

One night, we were all going to "Toys for Tots" and my neighbor's son was killed in a car wreck. He was one of those kids that was just put out on his own — you know, as long as you're not in my hair you're okay. I was the one he came to talk to when he didn't have anybody else to talk to. My great-grandmother died in November and he got killed in December and I didn't know how to deal with death to start with. The old you expect to die — she was eighty-seven. But somebody eighteen and you're just fourteen — it was a different world. I was hurting, I didn't know how to deal with it, and I remember being reprimanded for expressing my hurt.

Then in 1970 when I was still in high school I had a serious illness. I had a brain tumor. During my senior year I began having terrible headaches. The doctor was treating me for migraine headaches. I got to the point to where I had severe tunnel vision. He put me on codeine for headaches — that was a trip and a half. I didn't need alcohol any more. I started experiencing blackouts and I didn't know what was going on — I was in a total world outside of it.

I had gotten into a different religion and I was totally messed up about my religious beliefs. I had gone back to the church I was raised in. They started telling me that I was being punished by God and all this other stuff. The preacher wrote me a letter and told me that I would die because God was punishing me. I don't know what for, but this was my punishment, that I was going to die. It was my punishment for disobeying God, I guess. I used to have that letter, but I think I finally got rid of it. There are some weird religions out there, let me tell you.

Anyway, I went into a hospital near home. The old doctor who had been there for years, who had been my doctor forever, did my first spinal tap and detected the brain tumor. He diagnosed it, then sent me to the University of Kentucky Medical Center. He didn't have the sophisticated machinery that U.K. had so I went to U.K. and several more tests was done and what really happened was — God healed me.

I was supposed to go in on a Monday for further testing. When I got there — to U.K. — the tunnel vision was still pretty bad but other than that, I was fine. The headaches were gone, everything was gone. The doctors up there called it a phenomenon. They had the reports, the protein count in my spinal fluid and they had everything documented. They kept me four days. They did everything in the world to me — about poked my eye out, took pictures of my other eye. The dye liked to have killed me when they missed the vein and it come out under my skin. I was really sick that time.

I went back home and finished high school. I even went on our senior trip to Florida — Daytona Beach.

I couldn't think of anything that I had done to make God mad at me. As far as religion, it was more or less that I went because everybody went to church. But there was nothing there. I was walking around one of the biggest hypocrites that ever walked because I went to church — I did the formality. I was like the Pharisees in the Bible. I did the formalities of religion, but I didn't have a religion. I just had the pretense. I was what we call a Sunday Christian.

After high school I lived at home and worked on the farm. I

graduated when I was seventeen and you can't get much of a job until you're eighteen. I did a stint at college. I went to Tennessee Tech but I just stayed drunk — even in the daytime in the dormitory. I was in college, living in the dorm, but it just wasn't what I wanted to do. To me, it was just like being farmed out again — that was the impression that I had. I didn't get into any trouble. See, that's really been my biggest problem. I never got in trouble, even when I was drinking, even later in life — I never got in trouble. I only stayed at college a quarter then I went home. Then there was the usual bit with my Dad. I wanted to leave home and do what I wanted to do.

I got a job as a clerk in a store and I didn't drink then. I straightened up for a while — for a pretty good while. I worked as a clerk at a store and then I started working at factories where I would put in shift after shift.

I got married in between this time. I was nineteen. He was two years younger than I was. We grew up together. So when he graduated from high school, we got married. Now I know it was to get away from home.

I was working and he was farming his parents' farm. Then we both started working at the factory and we worked together there for two years; then he quit to farm full time. To me the farm was worth giving up everything for because that was what I wanted. I was pregnant, too, while doing farm work. I milked cows until I was eight months pregnant with Sarah. Then I got afraid — I was so big that I got afraid one of them cows would kick me so I had to quit milking. I was twenty-six and it was a difficult pregnancy. I started hemorrhaging at about seven months and had to stay in bed the last month which drove me nuts. I wasn't used to that. Being inside was bad enough, but being in bed was worse. I had to have an emergency C-section when Sarah was born.

When I was about seven months pregnant, the physical abuse had started. The verbal abuse had started practically after the marriage — after the "I dos" were said. When I was pregnant, he'd slap me — but that wasn't anything like what I was to face later on. Looking back now, I know he was never faithful to me, but I didn't know it then.

He had started working for the police department and I was

working the farm. Things were just continually getting worse. The December after Sarah was born I started working for the Soil Conservation Service — one of those fluff jobs — you answered the phone a half day Monday and Wednesday and all day Friday. I started reading manuals for the SCS and then more or less formed my own job which ended up being full-time. I started a district newsletter and I got featured at the state level two or three times. I had been in meetings with governors and senators. I was pretty good, you know. I was super-mom — trying to keep the farm and be a mother and work too.

During this time I was drinking only at night and on weekends. When the physical abuse had started, I started drinking again. He drank all the time. You know, you can't live with a drunk unless you are drunk, too. I drank to be a part of what his life had become, or what I thought he wanted. And I liked to drink — always had.

You know, I think I was a workaholic long before I was an alcoholic. The only thing that I had even as a child was the work. That's why I became the responsible child — I was always there. I took my shift when my grandmother was sick. I was fourteen when my great-grandmother was sick and in the hospital and I took my shift at the hospital just like the rest of them. This was my only self-worth — the only thing I could hold on to. I liked that part and you know, that's not a wrong value. The way that I interpreted it was wrong.

When my grandmother died, I picked up where my grandmother had left off — I started taking over the farm bit by bit from my grandfather. I was working two farms, plus the work at home and at the office also. Our farm was really my husband's dad's farm, but we built a house on it and owned the house and an acre of ground.

Then in 1984 we bought a farm in an adjoining county, which was supposed to be a new start for us. It was a one hundred and twenty acre dairy farm. We went through the FHA to finance it. We were one hundred thousand dollars in debt. We had most of our equipment bought and paid for by this time and had a pretty good start on the cattle. But, this new farm was going to be a new beginning — things were going to be different. My husband really wanted this farm. Looking back now, I believe he wanted to totally isolate me more because he was losing control of me and he was trying to regain it. By moving to this new farm, I would not have a job, I would be totally isolated from my family. Things were so bad with us. A few family members still came to see me but they knew that it only made things worse if they came so they didn't come often.

The physical abuse was still going on and becoming more evident because I couldn't hide the bruises any more. When it first started they were pretty easy to conceal by wearing long sleeves or hiding them under my clothes. But with the first black eye that I couldn't explain, it was getting increasingly harder to hide. He was getting harder to defend. You know, I was still putting up this front that everything was okay — that nothing was going on. It was very important to me that nobody found out what was really going on with us. At one point I had decided that he could live in our new farm and I would stay in my house on our old farm because part of me still didn't trust him. But his parents wanted the house so they bought it and I signed the deed and I moved to the new farm with him. Sarah had started to school. After we moved, I took her back home to school and drove back and forth every day for a year. Later Sarah started school near our new farm, but I couldn't leave her with him at any time because he was abusive to her too.

Things went down hill — the snowball effect. I quit work, my grandfather died, and in May my husband's girlfriend moved in with us along with her daughter and her daughter's three kids. Well, he wouldn't hit me when people were around. I am a survivalist and this was a survival technique for me — to let them live with us. I was sick from the word go. And, at this point in time, I had started carrying a thirty-eight everywhere I went. I was that afraid — I had my thirty-eight in my hip pocket and I slept with it under my pillow. He was threatening me and I was living in the same house with him. I knew he was going to kill me sooner or later. I lived like this for years!

At one point I went to the preacher of the church I was going to. That was a wrong move. You just end up getting talk splattered all over everywhere. Well, my husband found out that I'd been to the preacher talking and I can remember he had me down in the floor and he was choking me and he said, "Now call your God to get me." I'm scared even now that God's going to strike him down.

I was never at peace — constantly on guard. He wasn't as bold until he got me away from my family. Once I just gave up and said, "Look, if you're going to kill me, kill me and get it over with." I had had all I was going to take but I didn't think of leaving during this time. I had nowhere to go. I was too ashamed to go home. That was really stupid but I was too ashamed because I had failed. It showed another failure for me. And when I had asked for what I thought should have been help from my preacher, help wasn't there and I was afraid to trust anybody else after that.

Well, you make your bed, you lay in it. That's what I've been taught. I hope people aren't teaching that to their children now but maybe they are. There is no way I would ever want my daughter to feel like she ever had to put up with a boyfriend hitting her. I would say, "You dump him right now — get rid of him."

Well, we were all one happy little commune, I guess you'd call it. Except, I was doing all the work and they were out all hours of the night carousing and everything else. Some very unsavory people started coming around the house — these were people you didn't want to mess with. I finally told him, "Look, you want to live your life, live your life, but you're going to do part of the work around here. I'm tired of it." So I started making them milk at night. I milked every morning and they would milk at night — which allowed me more drinking time is about what it boiled down to, because that's all I done.

I remember Sarah begging me to leave and I was saying, "I can't. We can't make it on our own. You just don't understand how life is." And I kept thinking things would get better — things would change. That's the age-old hope.

I remember the last beating he gave me before his girl friend moved in. I had been drinking and he started letting everybody know that I was drinking. He aimed to kill me or beat me up and then to throw me in front of a car down on the main road. He was going to say that I was drunk and walked out in front of the car. That was his full intention but that was one time I fought back. I picked up a shovel and I hit him then ran back into the house. That night I was not drinking and he poured beer and whiskey on me so I would have the odor. He had already spread these rumors around that I was drinking so all he had to do was push me out in front of a car.

Well, there's safety in numbers so I let his girlfriend move in with us. I didn't know it at the time, but he was secretly moving what he wanted from off the farm — hiding it — equipment and stuff. He was getting everything situated to where he would control everything he wanted so he could leave. And he did. There was an altercation. He was going to run off and take Sarah and he was drinking, but I tore the wires off my car so he couldn't leave with her. He called his parents and told them I was drinking and trying to kill him. They come and got Sarah and when they took her, something in me snapped. The kid was my life — she was the reason I had done all the work. Well, when they left with her it wasn't ten minutes before he went and got his girlfriend and brought her to the house. I walked to the barn where they were and I told him that I had every intention of killing him and that I would if he came in the house. I went in the house and I barricaded all the doors but one and sat there watching "Seven Brides for Seven Brothers" all night long on the Disney Channel. I was waiting for him to show up and I would have killed him. He didn't show up. He knew better. Then my mother had an accident and I had to go home to take care of her. He tried to file for divorce on grounds of desertion but that didn't work. I wouldn't give him a divorce. It was a matter of pride.

So I went back to him. The next day, they left for Florida — left me there with seventy-some head of cattle and nothing — not even a hammer to fix the fences with. He had hid all our stuff at his mom and dad's farm. I was left with nothing but movies and that's what I did most of the time — just watch movies. Not even a hammer to fix the fences.

I managed to sell the cattle and pay the bank mortgage so I come out okay on that one. I put the farm in the hands of a realtor. My mom had bought a farm off of my grandfather's estate and I could live in a house there. I had to declare a legal residence to get my daughter back — she was eight years old at this point. I was glad I got her away from his mom and dad because it was a one-sided thing. But, really, I wasn't in any shape to be an adequate influence on her life.

Well, my husband was still in Florida so I went in and filed for divorce. I went for a no-fault divorce because I didn't want anything that was going on coming out in court. When I filed for divorce, he came back. His girlfriend dumped him in a motel in Louisville and he called me and I went and got him. Just like the dutiful wife, I took him back. The farm was still in the realtor's hands and he moved back in there while I was still living in the house my mom had bought from my grandfather's estate. I got to wondering if his girlfriend was living out there with him so when I was a little bit tipsy I got my brother to take me out there. We went in — he was drunk — and he pulled a shotgun on us. He aimed to kill us both that night. My brother whipped him and took the gun away from him. My husband later told his parents that we went in on him and beat him up. It was a vengeance thing — all vengeance.

He stayed out there on the farm until his girlfriend's daughter's boyfriend broke his ankle in three places. My husband called me at two in the morning to come take him to the doctor, and I made his parents go with me. Well, I stayed with him three days in the hospital and took him home with me to my house and took care of him for three more weeks. I ended up with two black eyes and a fractured jaw and — well, that was it! After that, it was just straight down to the bottle as deep as I could go. I drank to try to cope. I drank to hide.

But I did start counseling at Comp Care. I had my counselor convinced that I only drank on weekends and I only drank at night to help me sleep — it was better than taking nerve pills. Because I had grown up seeing Mama so controlled by nerve pills, I didn't want to do that. I was staying locked up in my house for weeks on end, drunk. My dad had Sarah at this time. I would just shut myself up in the house. It was the only form of suicide that I could do — I didn't have enough guts to blow my brains out. I was afraid — afraid that I'd mess it up. I knew sooner or later the law of averages would get me. As long as I was drunk, I didn't have to think about it — I didn't have to care. Nothing was important any more.

Finally, my counselor decided that I needed to go into a treatment center on a Monday. I had been drunk for about two weeks — had had two meals and got sober for two days so I could go get more. Then it just hit me — I was afraid to get better. I mean, if I didn't have this pity to draw off of, I might really have to do something. At that point in my life I could not see any reason to live. I was thirty-four; I had wasted sixteen years of my life — I had nothing to show for these sixteen years except my daughter. So I decided to make sure that I had one glorious weekend before they sent me to the treatment center — go out in a blaze of glory, as the song says.

I got a gallon of Early Times whiskey, which was my drug of preference, and a full bottle of Miloril from my doctor and I planned to make my daughter mad enough at me that she wouldn't care if anything happened to me. And, I was going to kill myself with the Miloril and the alcohol. Well, I wrote suicide notes and hid them and then I made her mad at me. This was on a Friday night.

I woke up the next morning at Crossroads, a treatment center in London, Kentucky. I didn't even know where London was at. Apparently on Friday night one of the counselors at the treatment center called me to come to the center. I told them, "I am drunk and I can't drive. I can't come up there." They said, "Don't you have a family member to bring you?" Sarah must have known something was going on because she grabbed the phone and said, "Yeah, she's got a sister and she'll be there." I don't remember much about what went on but my family took me to Crossroads.

I didn't have any idea where London, Kentucky, was at — which was a blessing in disguise because had I known where it was at, I would have been gone. I would have left. I was about one hundred miles from home. I had no medical insurance or anything and Crossroads was the only one that took people that didn't have insurance. It's a state run treatment center that only takes ten women at a time. They had twenty-six men and ten women.

Well, this first time I went in, it was for a twenty-eight day program. To me, it was like being in jail; I thought it was like a lockup but it's not. You're not locked up — you can leave at any time. But it was the closest thing to jail I had ever been in and I can remember thinking, "Well, here I am in a treatment center for drinking." I thought, "I have worked hard, I partied hard" — and it was just a way of life for me. I didn't know what Alcoholics Anonymous was or anything — I thought AA was the auto club. They kept running around saying "Don't forget AA tonight." And I thought, "What in the world is the auto club coming in here for?" I mean, I was dying and here were these people running around with smiles on their faces.

That's when I first met Mama Lucille. She was my counselor at Crossroads. She was something else. She was the warden, her and Dennis. You know, as I went through the program I thought, "Okay, well, this will get people off my back. I'll go home and a little later on I'll resume life back the way it was." I never really accepted the fact that I was an alcoholic because I had never been in trouble with the law and alcoholics are people that have all this trouble. I'm not a bad lady. I learned later that for everything you think you haven't got — just add "yet" to it. Because sooner or later, it'll catch you when you have this disease.

That's when I met this terrific man, who was in there being treated, too. I had come out of a rotten marriage where I had gotten left for a woman who was a dog — she had been on the streets since she was thirteen. But she was being used just as much as I was. Anyway, I had finally met someone that thought I had a brain — which I never thought I had. He was nice, kind; he told me I was beautiful. After we left the treatment center, he moved in with me. I went back home and he went with me. We lived together; we farmed; we did odd jobs farming and we had some good times in general. We both ended up drinking again. The only problem was, this time I was six months pregnant and this time I knew there was no excuse for it. I definitely had a problem. I called my dad to take me back to Crossroads. I remember walking in and Lucille was there to greet me again. I was crying so hard and I said, "You know, I know I don't belong here." She looked at me and she said "You're not starting this b.s. over again. You're here and you know you belong here."

They really weren't supposed to take me because I was pregnant but they did. This time my ulcer started bleeding and I ended up for three days in the hospital. I was severely anemic and my mind functions were not too great at this time. I stayed at Crossroads thirty-five days because they were working on trying to find a place for me to go other than back home. I definitely couldn't go back and here I was, thirty-five years old and homeless. Lee, the man I had been living with, ended up in jail.

Lee came back to Crossroads for treatment and I moved in at the Family Life Center. From there I would drive back and forth to the treatment center for AA meetings because I didn't know any places besides the treatment center you could go for AA. I got counseling there too and really got to work out a bunch of problems. It was fantastic. The Family Life Center had never took an alcoholic woman before. I was kind of "new ground" for them. I didn't know about these people and I didn't know how to act around them. To be honest, they didn't know what to do with me. I had never even been that far away from home. But it worked out real good. You know, everybody is different. Everybody's drinking patterns are different — but I knew I had already reached the point in my life that the only thing I was looking at was death. It was change or die.

Lucille had gotten me started seeing a doctor in Corbin. I hadn't even been to a doctor until that point. I drove myself back and forth to the doctor. I always managed to keep gas money as I could work a little on the side at this time. I was staying sober during all this time and everything was working out fine. My son, David, was born the first of February — repeat Caesarean. But something went wrong during the spinal block and my blood pressure dropped too fast and I started hyperventilating and then it dawned on me that I had made no plans about what to do with my baby if anything should happen to me. Then, things started making sense. I did have a choice in life! But it's not been easy. None of it's been all that easy.

I took David and we went back to the Family Life Center. They let me work out my rent, and I took on odd jobs — whatever I could do. They signed me up for AFDC and Sarah was able to join us in March. I hadn't planned on bringing her up there with me until the end of the school year but she got afraid of her daddy — he had started drinking pretty bad and was threatening her. We stayed there until May. I think I was very fortunate in that I had that time to work on a lot of stuff that was bothering me. It was a healing time and it helped me to get a stronger foothold.

In May we moved out into a federal housing project in Mount Vernon. I was still going to AA and working my program. I helped get another AA started in the Catholic church at Mt. Vernon. This was the first time I had had neighbors in my life because I had always lived in the country. I had a realization of how you are looked on when you live in these places. I enrolled Sarah in school, but when you're in a shelter or housing project, there's a tendency for the school to treat your children as throw-aways. She'd get no grade card so I didn't know what she was doing at school. I would ask and they'd say, "Oh, she's doing fine." You know, like, "Why bother — she's not going to be here that long anyway." I guess the tendency to feel that way was understandable — but it's highly prejudiced.

That's what I ran into, living in the housing project. So, I found a farmhouse out in the country, an older farmhouse and they wanted one hundred dollars a month for it. I could swing it on AFDC and picking up odd jobs. It was more serene. I'm just not the kind of person who functions very well in a closed environment. We moved out in December and looking back, that was not a great time to move — I should have picked a warmer time. We didn't have a lot, but God's always provided what I need. When I stop and look back now I can see how His hand was just guiding, how each little building block it took to get just that one step further.

Well, the first year — maybe a year and a half — I couldn't have held down a job. I had too much I was working on, getting too much sorted out. There was still a lot of pain left to deal with, but it gets easier with time.

Then the New Opportunity School came along. Judy Wilson, my friend — my straight friend, which means that she is not an alcoholic but married to an alcoholic — said, "I've sent off for this information about this program and when I get it back, I'll let you know." I guess she got tired of me griping about "Oh, I want to do something but I don't know what to do." When she saw the ad in the paper she supposedly sent off for information for herself. When the information packet came back she said, "I think you'd really enjoy doing this. I'll call them and have them send you one also."

So I got the packet back and I had to write an essay about why I want to go to the school and I thought, "I can never express these feelings — I have these feelings, but getting them out is hard." I knew what I didn't want in life and I knew only one thing I wanted in life — I knew I wanted to give back. I don't want to be a taker.

So I filled out the application and sent it back, but I thought,

132

"It won't do any good." Well, I got accepted and I came to the New Opportunity School and, well, everything just connected, just jelled. I can't explain it. It was like I walked in and it was total acceptance. I had never experienced that. I immediately felt accepted. It was definitely a time of self-analysis. The strangest thing was that I had never felt like I belonged anywhere — I don't know if it was from moving so much when I was a kid — but I knew where I belonged now. People thought I did have some good ideas — and I wasn't going to get my head chewed off or I wasn't going to get killed if I opened my mouth. The people at the school were easy to care about.

It was during that time that I knew I wanted to go into nursing. I had had no experience working in the hospital but had taken care of some elderly relatives. We took care of them at home but when they were in the hospital, I was there with them. I always admired nurses and working in the Berea Hospital during the New Opportunity School was what really made me know more about what nursing was.

Soon after the New Opportunity School I enrolled in a nursing program at the vocational school. David will attend school for a half a day, then he'll go to a babysitter for the other half while I go to school. I can get help with paying for his child care through the new JOBS program for mothers on AFDC. My fourteen year old daughter is living with me; she's in high school and goes by bus into Mt. Vernon.

I get nervous and anxious because I really want to get started in school and I'm afraid that the more time that goes by, the more that I'm losing brain cells. I already blew all my math brain cells away! But, if I get a job now rather than go to school, in twenty years I'm not going to be any better off. As long as I have some education, nobody's going to take that from me.

You know, God has always furnished me with a way to do what I need to do.

(Beverly has just completed LPN training and is applying for jobs throughout Kentucky. She no longer receives AFDC and has been able to purchase her own home. Sarah is now married and living in her own home with her husband and Beverly's first grandchild. David is progressing well and will enter first grade this year. Beverly often gives speeches to various

groups encouraging other women to become the very best they can be. She says, "I firmly believe that as long as you put forth the effort, no matter what life has been for you, you will succeed.")

INTERVIEW METHODS

All interviews with the nine women were tape recorded and later transcribed. The length of the interviews varied from one and a half to three hours. In addition to the nine stories here, several other women were also interviewed but for a variety of reasons their stories were not used.

All interviews began with my talking to each woman about the book project and asking her for permission to tape her story for it. Each woman was told that she would have an opportunity to read her completed story and make any deletions and changes.

Although specific questions were asked all women interviewed, the topics varied throughout the interviews, depending upon individual situations and perceived significance of happenings in their lives.

I edited the lengthy transcriptions to place the material in chronological order, to give more continuity and clarity to the stories and to omit repetitious material. The words used here are the actual words of the women; the descriptions of their lives are their own.

J.S.

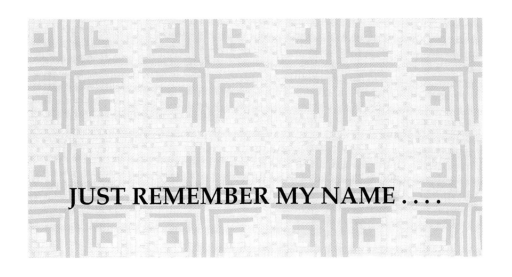

JUST REMEMBER MY NAME . . . .

Two years after her husband, John Stephenson, took the reins of Berea College in 1984, Jane Stephenson was still looking for a project. By nature, she was an activist in the tradition of other wives who had preceded her at the President's House on Chestnut Street, but she still had found no consuming cause to call her own. Her search ended rather abruptly one morning in the fall of 1986 — with a telephone call from her friend Gurney Norman, the writer and English professor at the University of Kentucky.

Norman was looking for help. He had a female friend facing a crisis. The middle-aged woman was going through a divorce; she was financially distressed; she had no marketable job skill; and she was on her own. Her problems were compounded by a debilitating lack of confidence. It was, of course, an increasingly familiar story, and it was especially so to Stephenson. Growing up in the mountains at Banner Elk, North Carolina, she had known a great many women like Norman's friend. She had worked with people like them as a specialist in adult education and the wife of an Appalachian scholar. Theirs was one of the recurring tragedies of the mountains, the kind of lives that Loyal Jones once described as a trip on a "circular sorghum mill." Norman's friend was still on Stephenson's mind the following day and she spoke with her husband about it. Later on John Stephenson received a call — this one from the California-based Educational Foundation of America. The organization had supported Berea programs in the past. It was completing its budget planning for the coming year, and its officials wanted to know whether Berea had a special need where the foundation could be helpful.

John Stephenson answered with a question of his own. Would the foundation be interested in a program to help low-income women desperately needing jobs? It was.

Thus was born the New Opportunity School for Women.

Facing a deadline less than a week away, Jane Stephenson put together a formal proposal. Using Norman's friend as a prototype, she sketched an intense and ambitious program designed to instill self-esteem and confidence in women whose aspirations had been stillborn. It was a quixotic plan to help them believe that middle age was the beginning of their life, not the end. Six months later, in June of 1987, the new school welcomed its first students to the Berea campus.

Without fully realizing it even then, Stephenson had found her cause — as part of what is perhaps the most significant social movement in Appalachia during the last years of the twentieth century: the emerging of women. The New Opportunity School opened for business in the midst of a decade in which the collapse of the coal economy and revolutionary changes in technology shook the social order of the mountains. Unemployment in coal towns soared as men found themselves with job skills no longer needed in their native hills — and with attitudes and prospects irrelevant in the cities to which miners used to migrate. A generation of mountain men now finds itself "with attitudes and values no longer consistent with the modern world," says Ronald Eller, director of the Appalachian Center at the University of Kentucky. For them, migration to Cincinnati or Charlotte or Pittsburgh is no longer the option that it once was.

Consequently, efforts to bring about grass-roots community change are increasingly being led by women, who have assumed growing responsibility for the feeding, clothing, and maintaining of families. As employment of men stagnated or declined, robust numbers of women have joined the work force. Birth rates have plummeted. Three-fourths of the students now entering community colleges in the region are female. With divorce and single parenthood becoming acceptable, families headed by women are commonplace in the mountains, as they have long been in inner cities. Women, authorities such as Eller and Loyal Jones, retired director of the Appalachian Center at Berea, agree, are more willing than men to take risks to change their lives and to work for change in economically distressed mountain communities.

Their role has changed not only because the modern economy increasingly excludes men who once dug coal, but because feminism has begun to resonate in rural areas. The special problems of poor women have come into focus, inspiring self-help organizations such as Workers of Rural Kentucky, the Mountain Women's Exchange in Tennessee, the Appalachian Committee for Children, and the Mud Creek Health Clinic, some of them led by women once on welfare. The assumption of roles undreamed by earlier generations of mountain women so far only emphasizes the magnitude of the problems faced by women and children in distressed areas. A recent study by the University of Kentucky's Appalachian Center found that poverty among women, children, and the elderly "increased markedly" during the 1980s in the state's Appalachian counties. In the poorest communities, nine of ten children in families headed by women were found to be in poverty. In three census tracts, every single family headed by a female existed on an income below the national poverty level.

Although it has recently begun to consider younger applicants, the New Opportunity School was created for women who find the challenge of new roles most daunting. Except for modern conveniences, many are not much different from their mothers. Growing up in hard-pressed circumstances, many left school and married in their early teens, promptly began having children of their own, and shortly found themselves captives of the same cycle that controlled their parents. By the time they reach the Berea campus, many have been divorced, widowed, or both, subjected to physical or psychological abuse, and discouraged from harboring any notions of changing their lives.

It is not uncommon for the women to arrive with significant health problems or to receive their first examination for breast or cervical cancer when they arrive in Berea. "We find women with serious health problems," Stephenson said, "and we are convinced that it is because they have not had physical or mental health care over the years. They have no insurance, and so they have not gone to doctors. We see people not only who have never had pap smears or mammograms, but who have high blood pressure and pre-stroke conditions without being aware of it. One woman had a blood clot in her leg and probably would have died had she not come to the New Opportunity School."

But the school does not select its students on the basis of direct circumstance. Motivation is weighed as heavily as need. Stephenson and her allies are looking for women with the fortitude to change their own lives and a capacity to help others.

Having now graduated fourteen classes with a total of one hundred and sixty-six women from its three-week-long total immersion sessions, the school has seen seventy percent of its graduates — who must have a high school diploma or GED certificate upon enrollment — go on to find jobs or enroll in college. Three-fourths of them have come from families with a total income of less than ten thousand dollars. Impressive as they are, such statistics fail to do justice.

Consider some examples:

—Linda, a divorced mother of three, was working as a domestic and earning two dollars an hour folding clothes at a laundromat before she went to the school in 1988. She had neither a telephone nor an automobile. Food stamps and subsidized housing now belong to her past. Remarried, she has vaulted into the middle class, working as a respiratory therapist in a hospital in another state.

—Cheryl Estep finished the eighth grade, married at fourteen, and became a grandmother at thirty-five. She had never worked outside her house until shortly before she went to the school at Berea. Now she goes to a Carter County Adult Education Center and studies for her college admission examination.

—Alma Young, forty, who was "painting fences and digging ditches" three years ago, now studies biology at Ashland Community College.

The list goes on.

These before-and-after snapshots only hint at the magnitude

of the personal transformations the program has inspired. In many cases students have come from circumstances that can only be described as horrific. While studying for her high school equivalency certificate, Estep had to hide her books from her disapproving husband. Young, reared by her grandfather, did not learn until his death that her mother lived just across the mountain. Another woman's life had been so unhappy that she lay face down on the floor of the Boone Tavern at Berea the night before graduating from the New Opportunity School and sobbed at the prospect of returning home.

In the course of selecting one of the early groups, Stephenson learned that a North Carolina woman who had applied was virtually a prisoner in her home. Never married, she was approaching middle age still living with her parents, her life brightened only by a huge collection of paperback books given to her over the years. The parents so feared her going away to school that they intercepted her correspondence. In the end, she made it to the three weeks in Berea, but she returned to her parents and, tragically, died of an aneurism shortly thereafter.

How can a mere three weeks produce the kind of changes chronicled in the New Opportunity School's records?

The approach is inspired in its simplicity.

It is designed to instill a sense of self-worth. The women begin their mornings with an Appalachian Literature class and books such as *The Tall Woman* by Wilma Dykeman and Gurney Norman's *Kinfolks*. They go on to a seminar in computer basics, and sessions on resume and creative writing. They also explore the home-based possibilities of business. The women visit a cosmetologist and a hair stylist for a "makeover." They're outfitted in clothes suitable for office work and put at ease by faculty members whose own roots lie in the mountains. During the afternoons, they are dispatched to work as interns at offices on the college campus, at Berea Hospital, and in businesses in the town of Berea. There are evening seminars and weekend trips to museums in Louisville and Cincinnati.

Most of them arrive feeling lonely and even terrified at the prospect of what lies ahead. Jo Ann Hall, a Grayson, Kentucky, widow who graduated from the program and now runs a GED training program in Carter County, recalls that she ate nothing at the dinner beginning her session. If she had, she knew she would become sick to her stomach because she was so frightened.

Feeling horribly out of place on the Sunday evening before the beginning of classes, Estep, who applied at Hall's urging, began gathering her belongings for a retreat to Carter County. But Hall, knowing what her protege was going through, chose that crucial moment to call from Grayson with reassurances.

Estep stayed. Three weeks after the opening dinner where she had been too frightened to utter a sound, she stood and told her classmates and nearly one hundred guests that her life had been changed. She was going to get an education, she said, she was not turning back. A teary-eyed Jo Ann Hall was in the audience.

The experience is frightening not only because of the unknown but because it represents for many of the women a bold declaration of independence. Of those who come to the school, about one-third are married. As they set out upon a new existence, a good many of them, not surprisingly, decide to divorce their husbands. "We hope that does not happen," Stephenson says, "but, realistically, it does. Some know their marriages are ending, for whatever reason, before they come. Others discover while they are here that their marriages are not healthy."

For most of the women, the three weeks provide a profound experience in self-discovery. They spend hours in group and individual sessions with Anita Barker, director of counseling at Berea College Health Service. And by all accounts, they spend even more time sharing experiences with each other into the wee hours of morning.

For whatever reason, says Barker, the women have long since come to "understand and accept faulty messages that they are not worth very much. We try to teach them to think thoughts that are true and thoughts that are real. We encourage them to stop listening to the old voices."

On the first Monday when they begin their sessions with Barker, women like Estep come to the dramatic and monumentally comforting realization that they are not alone in feeling hopelessly trapped in their unsatisfactory existence.

"They talk about things and cry with each other about things they have never discussed before," said Barker, who grew up in modest circumstances in Bear Wallow, Kentucky. "They talk about things that they have kept hidden inside and pretended never happened. When they get together here, they are ready to be healed."

"Anita Barker has worked with me on the program," Jane Stephenson said. "She has been my right arm from Day One of the program. She's really great with the women. They respond to her and she helps them grow in self-esteem."

Berea was a natural place for such an undertaking, committed, as it has been since its founding, to serving the poor of the Southern Appalachians. Early in the century, health and literacy programs for remote mountain areas were high among its priorities. Borrowing from Danish folk schools, the college, for a quarter century, operated an Opportunity School where citizens could come and study whatever they liked each January. Over the years, it has stayed in touch with its rural surroundings through a variety of outreach programs. The Bond House, a Victorian residence that now serves as the offices for the New Opportunity School, also functions as headquarters of the Brushy Fork Institute, a community leadership program organized by John Stephenson.

"In the New Opportunity School we see one of the best traditions of rural America," says Gurney Norman, "the tradition of neighbors helping neighbors. It could succeed anywhere, but it has succeeded marvelously here because it is so grounded in traditions. Here, people will still help someone. So what Jane did was sort of flip a switch and all of this positive energy came forward."

During the early days, the New Opportunity School's assets were Stephenson and her personal computer in a little niche of the President's house. Her husband licked stamps and helped her with mailings to spread the word. When the first class arrived, both he and Norman joined the faculty, as did others from the Berea faculty. Wilma Dykeman became a regular, inspiring succeeding classes with stories of powerful and successful Appalachian women, as did Alex Haley, who, until his death in 1992, invited succeeding classes to his home in East Tennessee.

John Stephenson taught Appalachian Literature, introducing the women to powerful figures from their region. He chauffeured a school van taking them on their field trips to museums and to appointments for the haircuts and makeovers that braced their fragile confidence in themselves. During it all, he put them at ease so successfully that he came to be openly referred to as "Mr. Jane," a tribute to both the college president and his wife. Norman's composition workshop has succeeded in convincing the students that they are naturally articulate and that satisfaction and self-discovery are to be found in writing.

After going home, some graduates continue writing in a personal journal that they begin at the New Opportunity School. "That journal," says Cheryl Estep, "means more to me than anything I own."

They also write letters to Jane Stephenson and Anita Barker. "A day never passes that I don't hear from some of them," says Stephenson. "We do a newsletter two or three times a year, and we include excerpts from the letters, thus keeping the women in touch."

When Kathleen Perry got home to her house on Beaver Creek in Menifee County, Kentucky, she had decided to write a book. To help her out, her husband, Harold, who had postponed surgery so she could go to the school for three weeks, made her a computer table. On it, she wrote a column for the *Berea Register*, ending with a note to Jane Stephenson.

"Your faith has not been misplaced, " she wrote. "Just remember my name . . . you'll be hearing from me."

Rudy Abramson

Retired Washington, D.C., correspondent of the *Los Angeles Times*, Rudy Abramson is author of *Spanning the Century*, a biography of *W. Averell Harriman*, published in 1992.

(Reprinted with permission from the APPALACHIAN HERITAGE, Summer, 1994, pp. 8 - 17)